DINOSAUR
Coloring Book

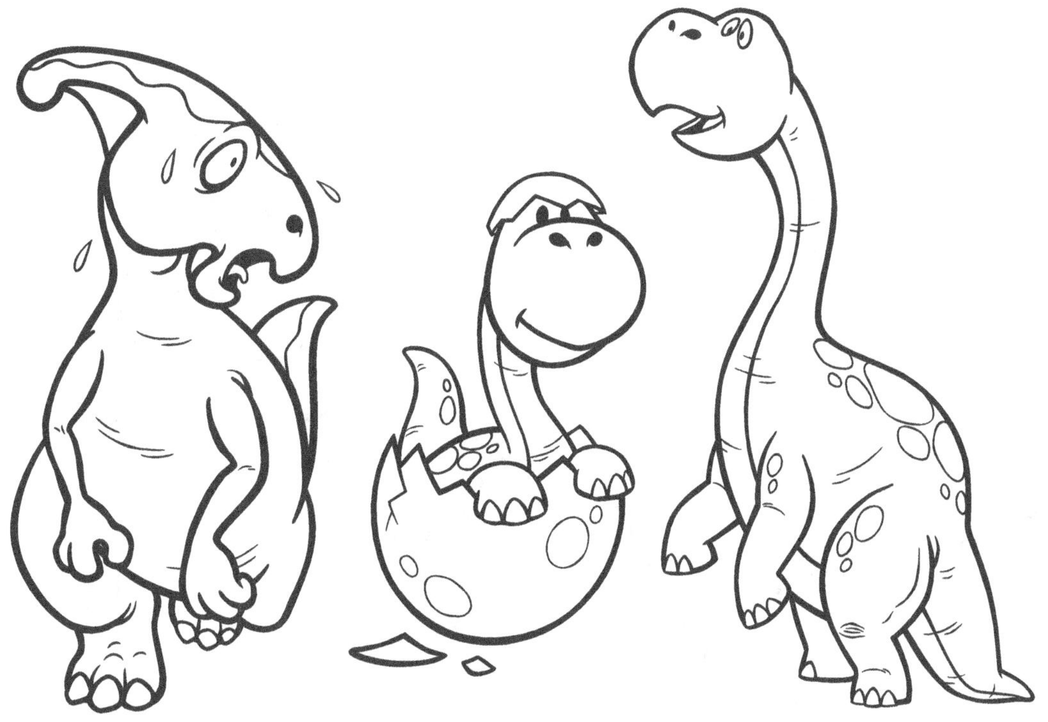

This Book Belongs To:

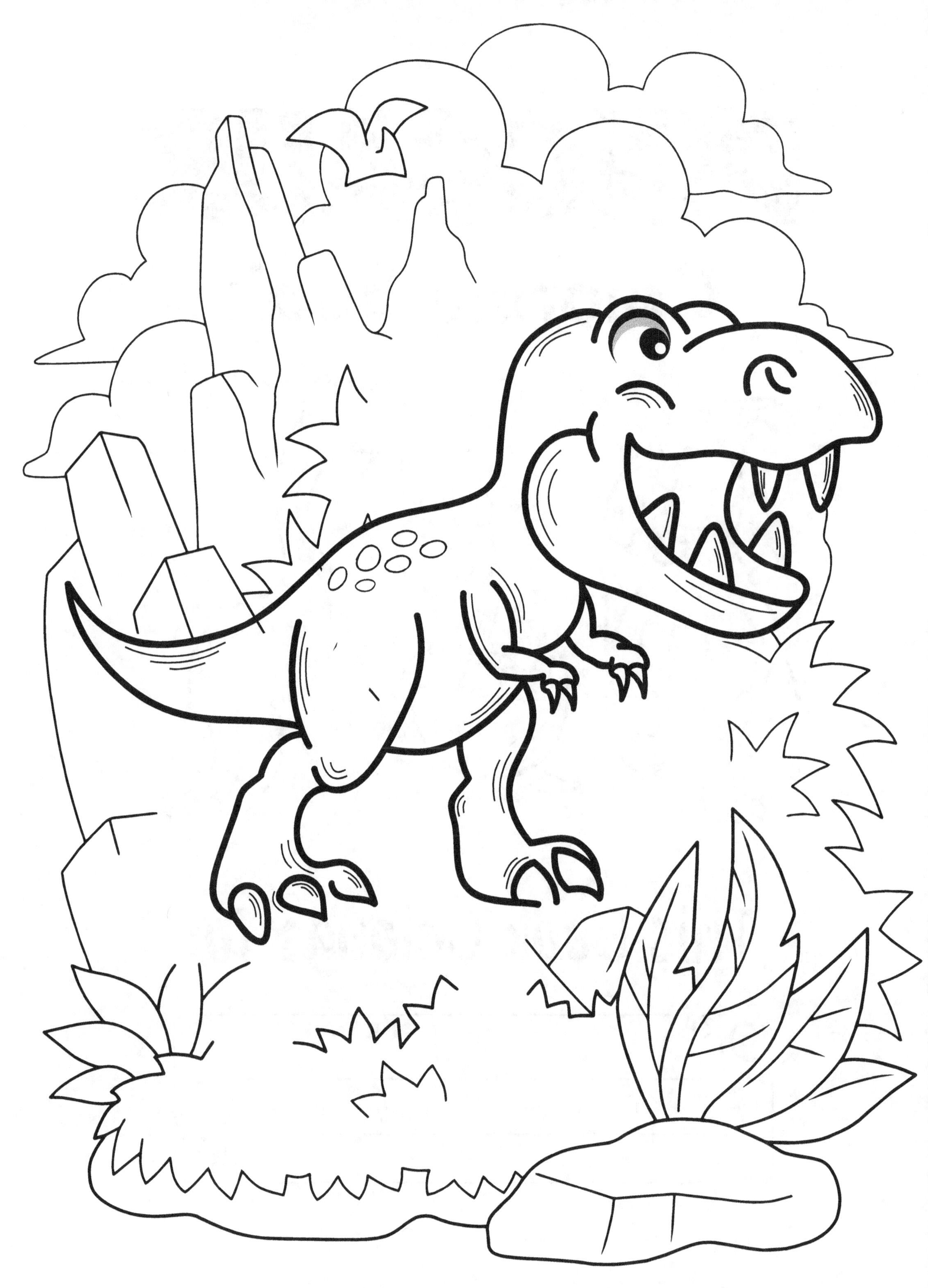

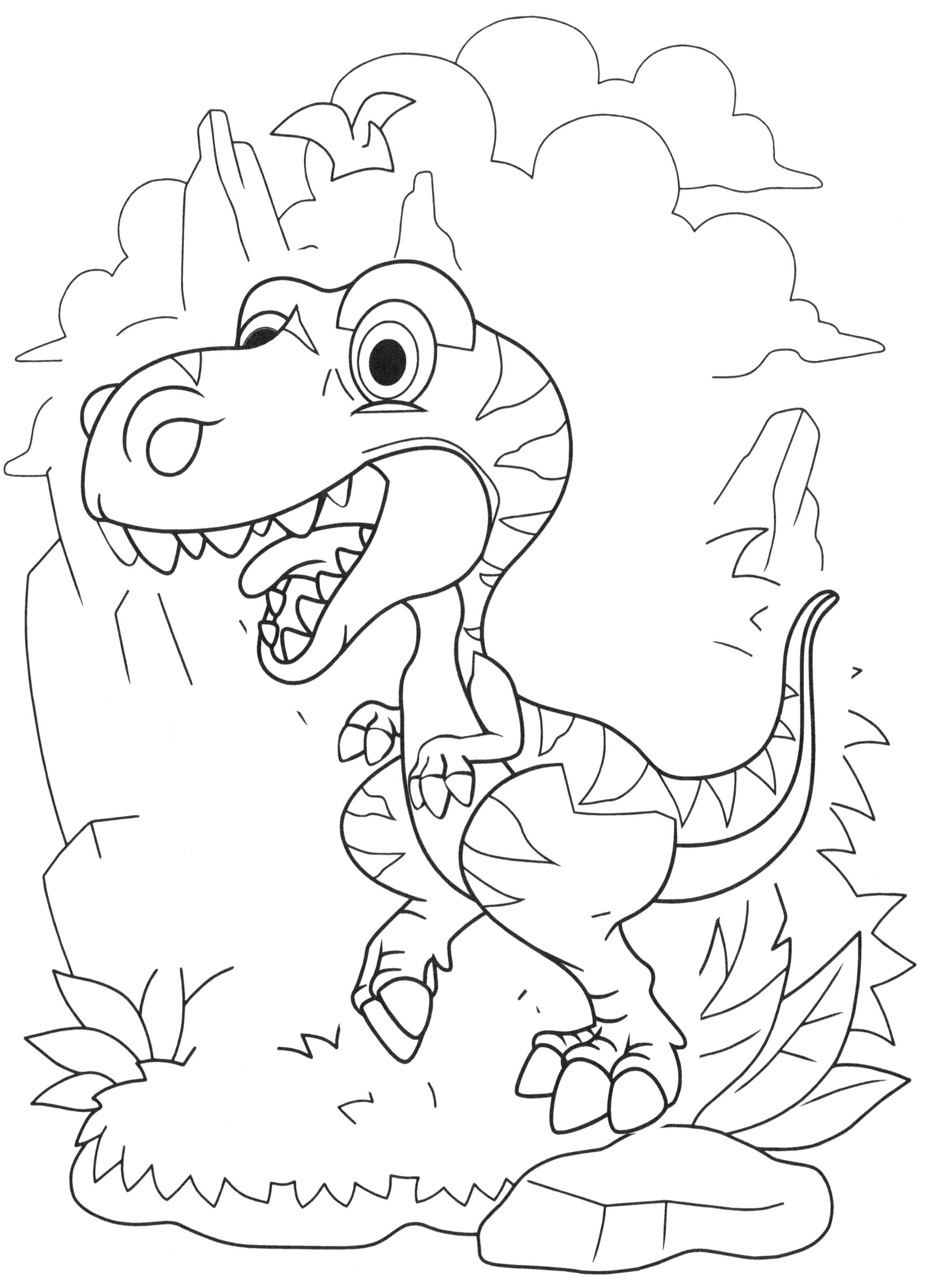

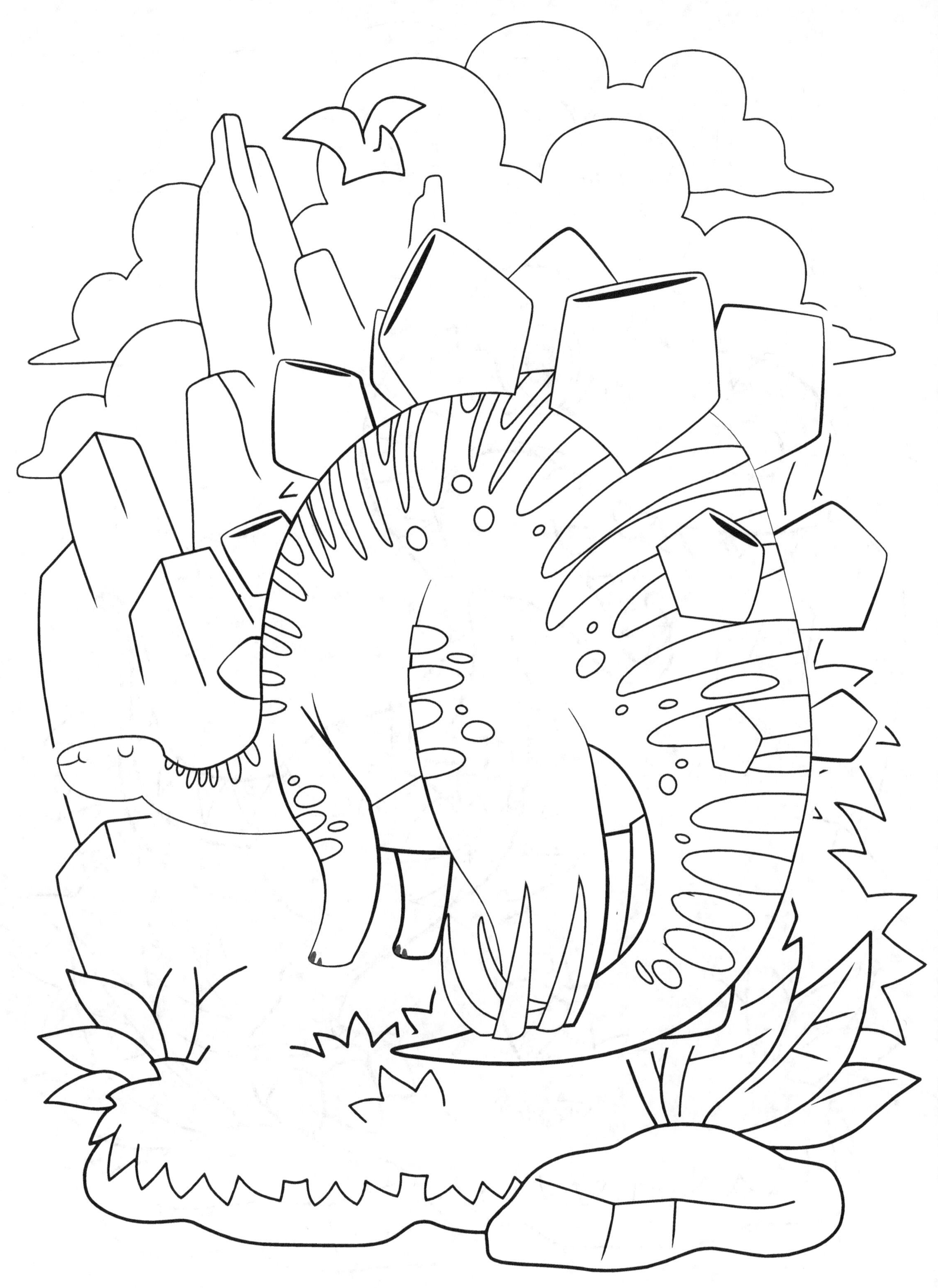

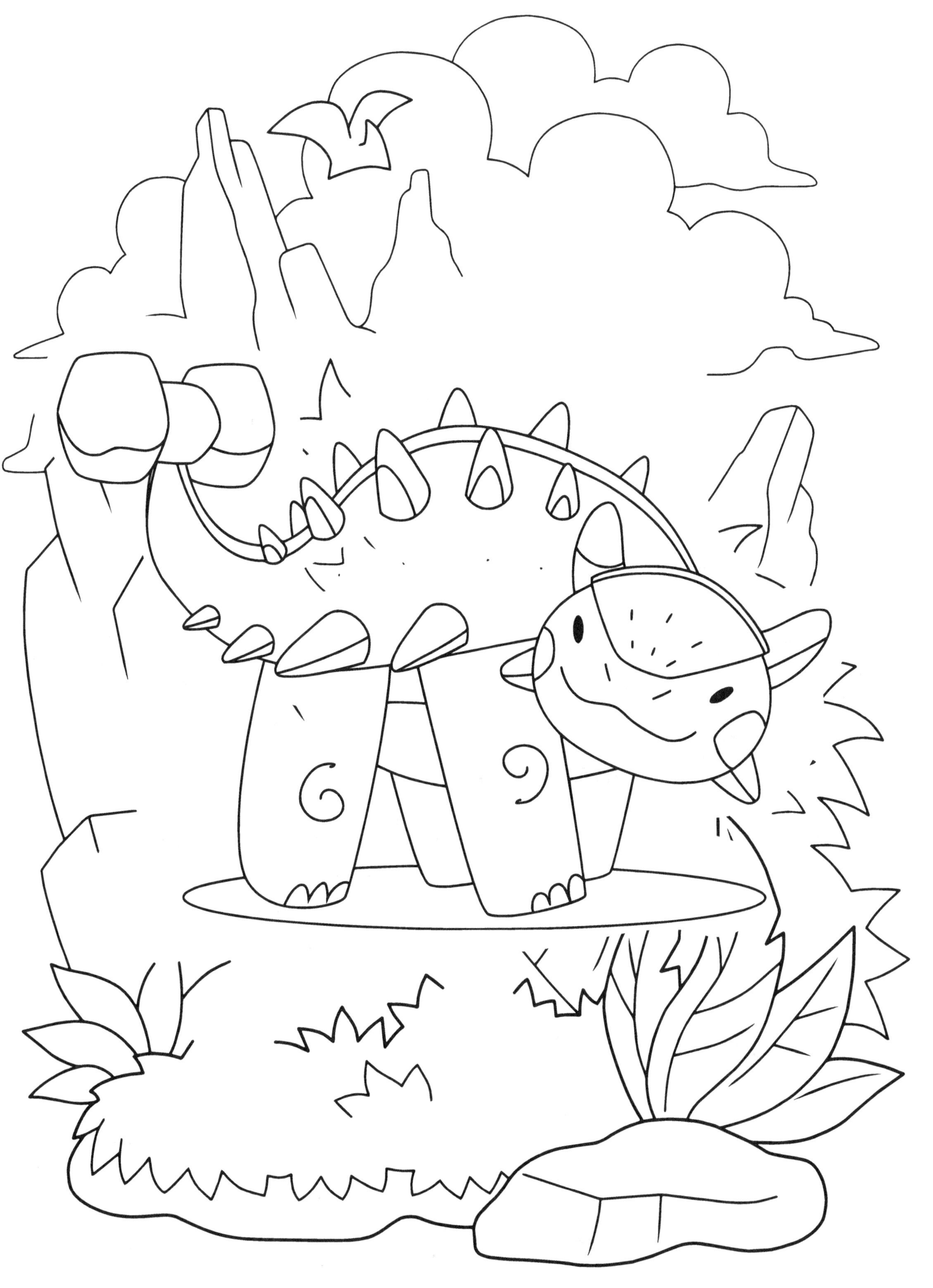

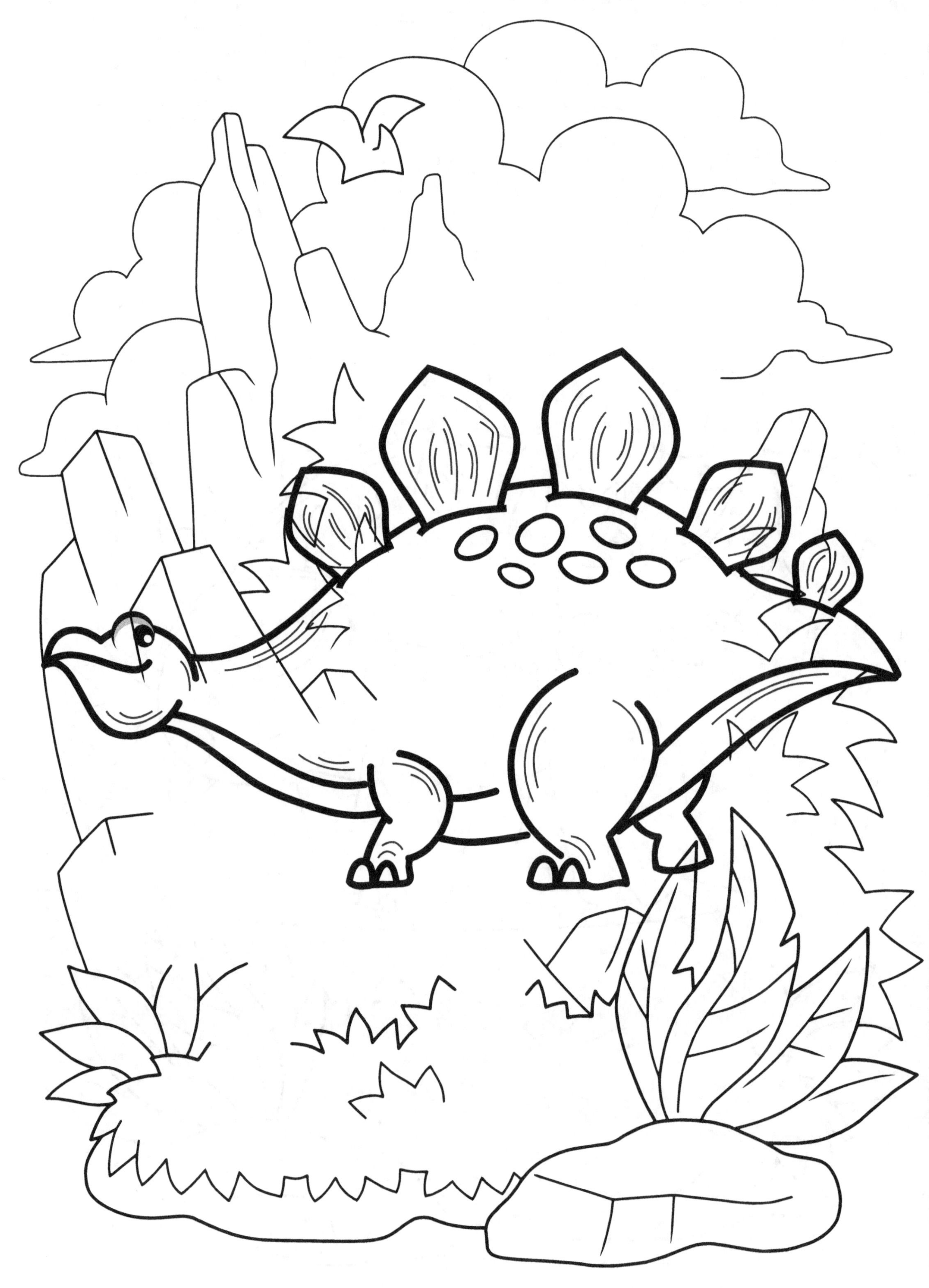

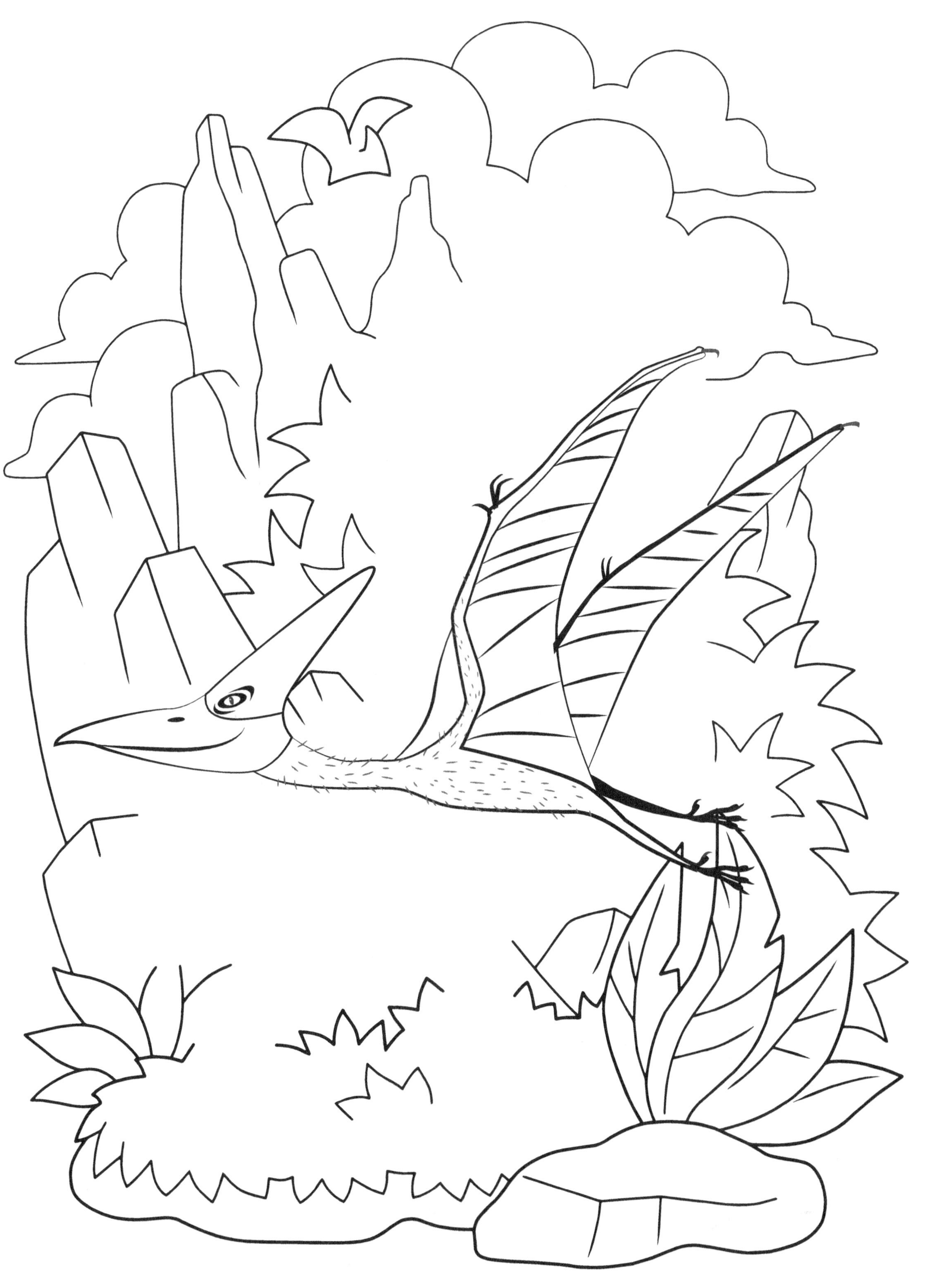

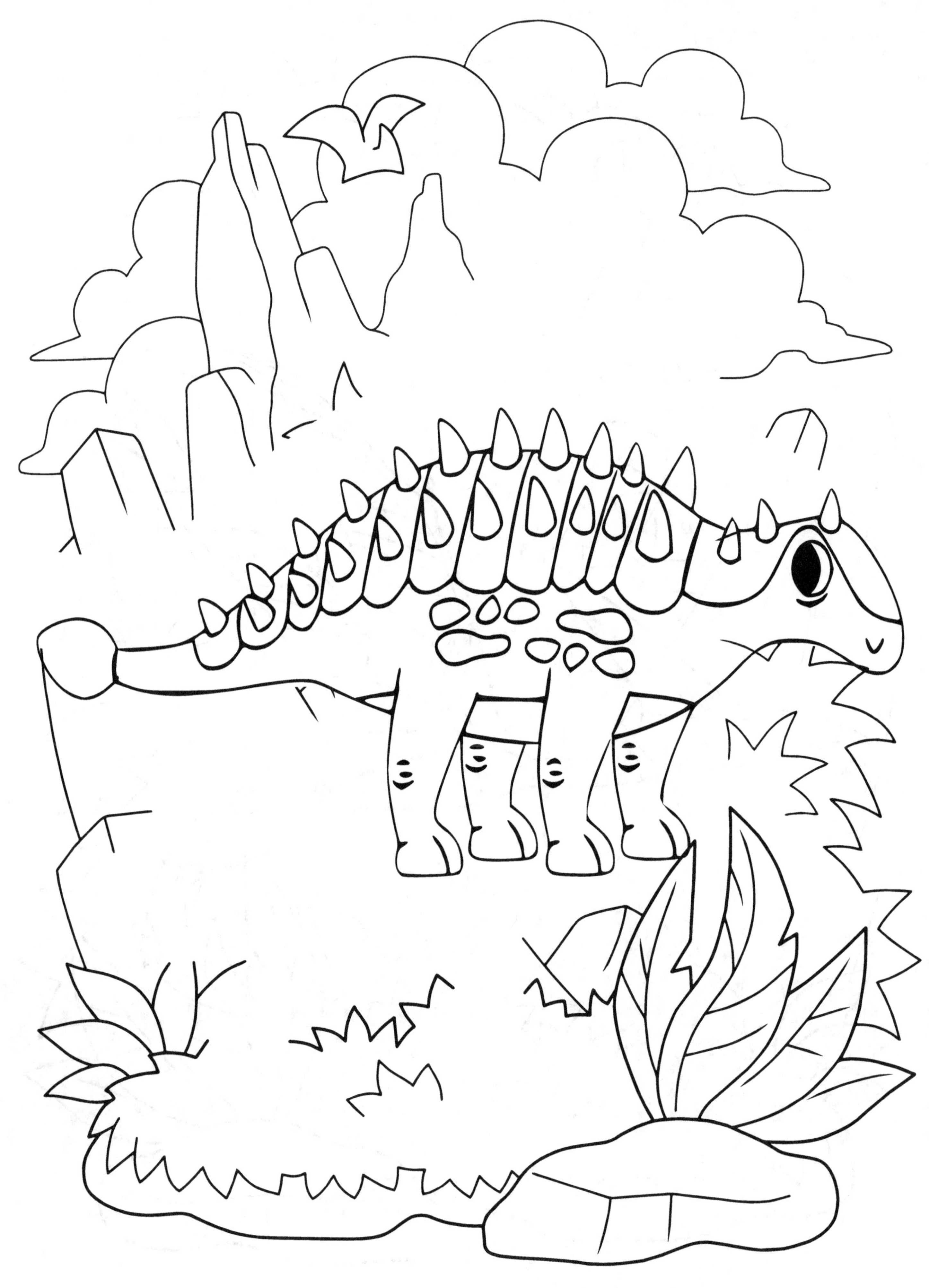

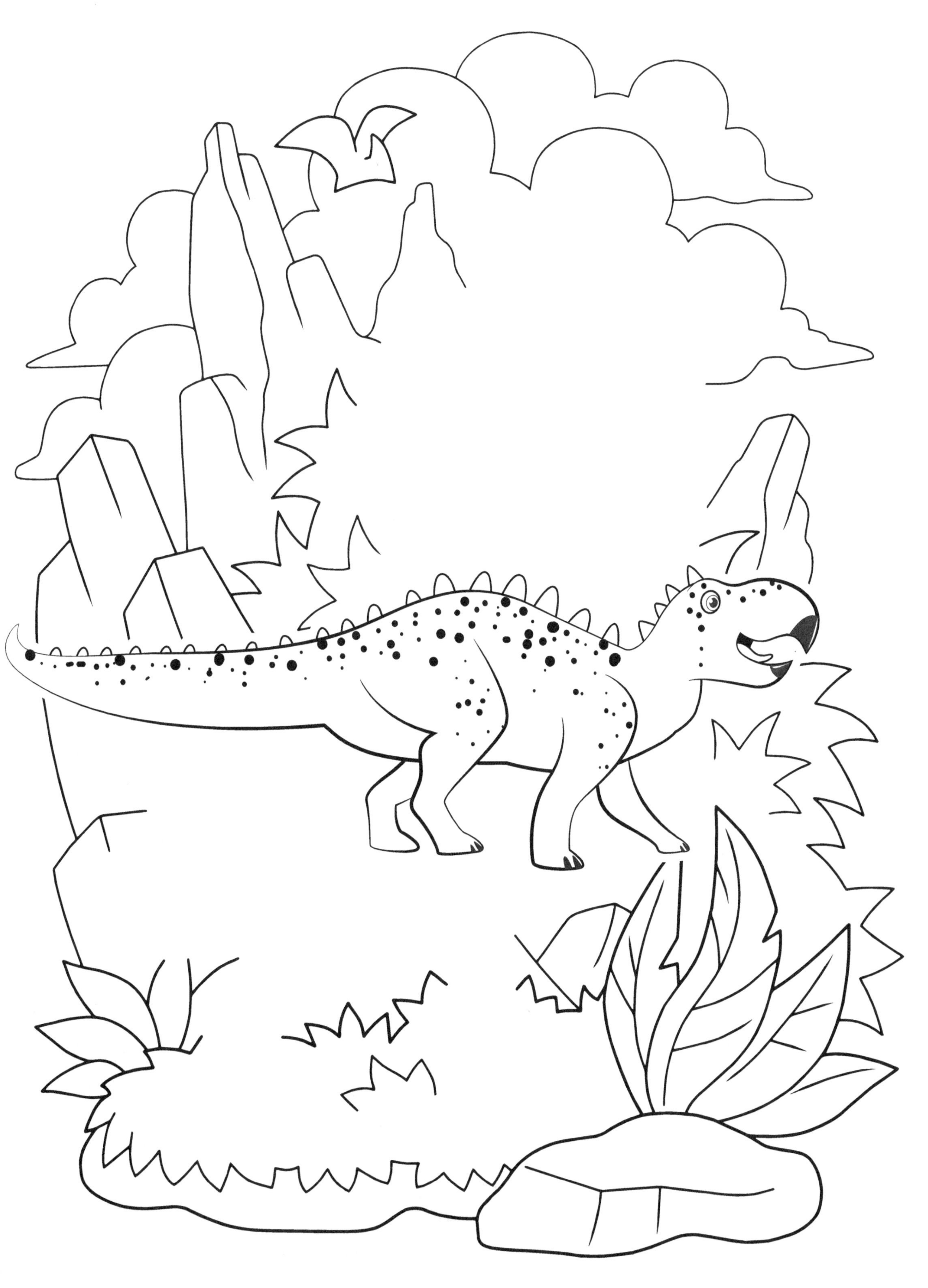

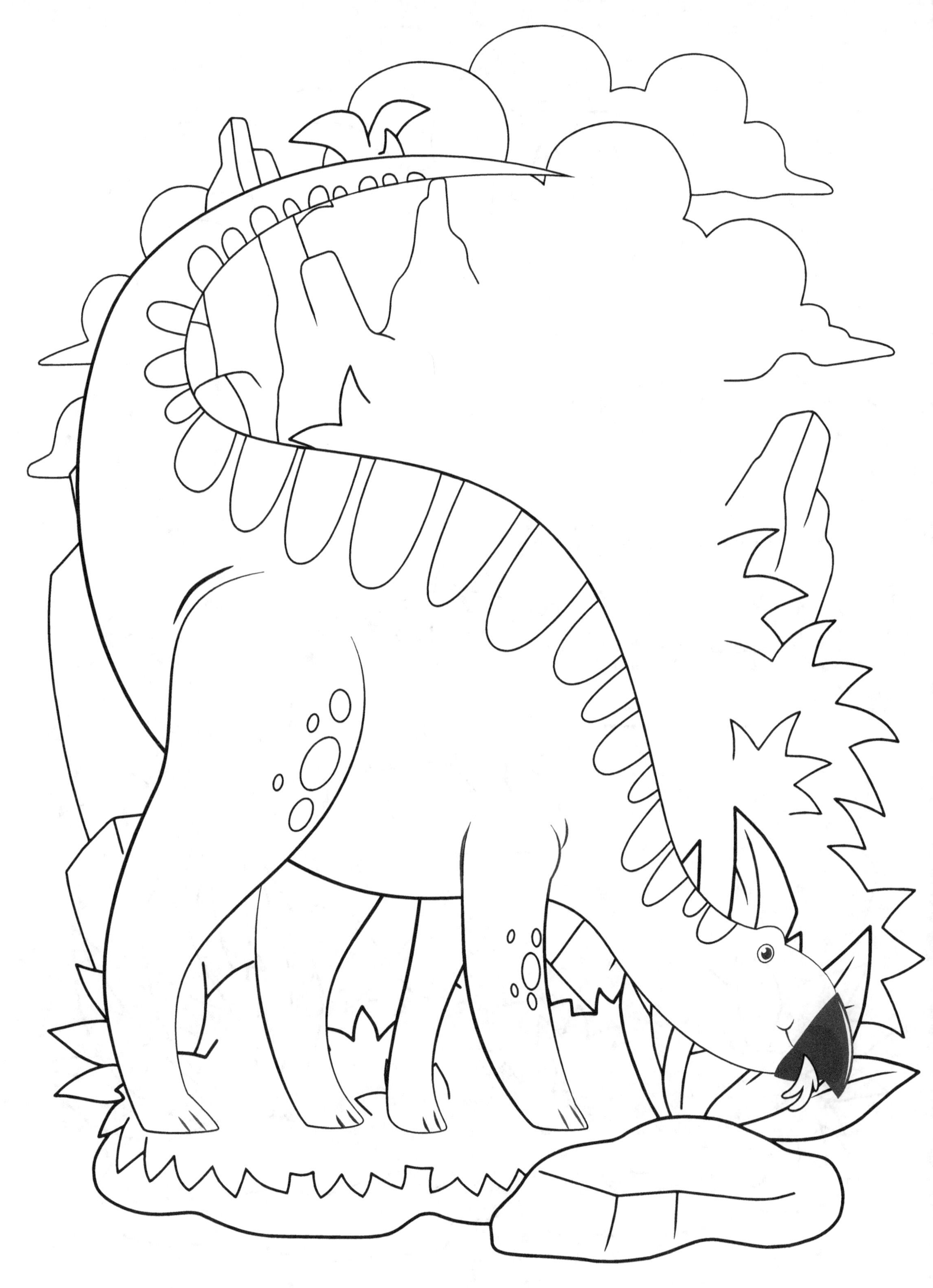

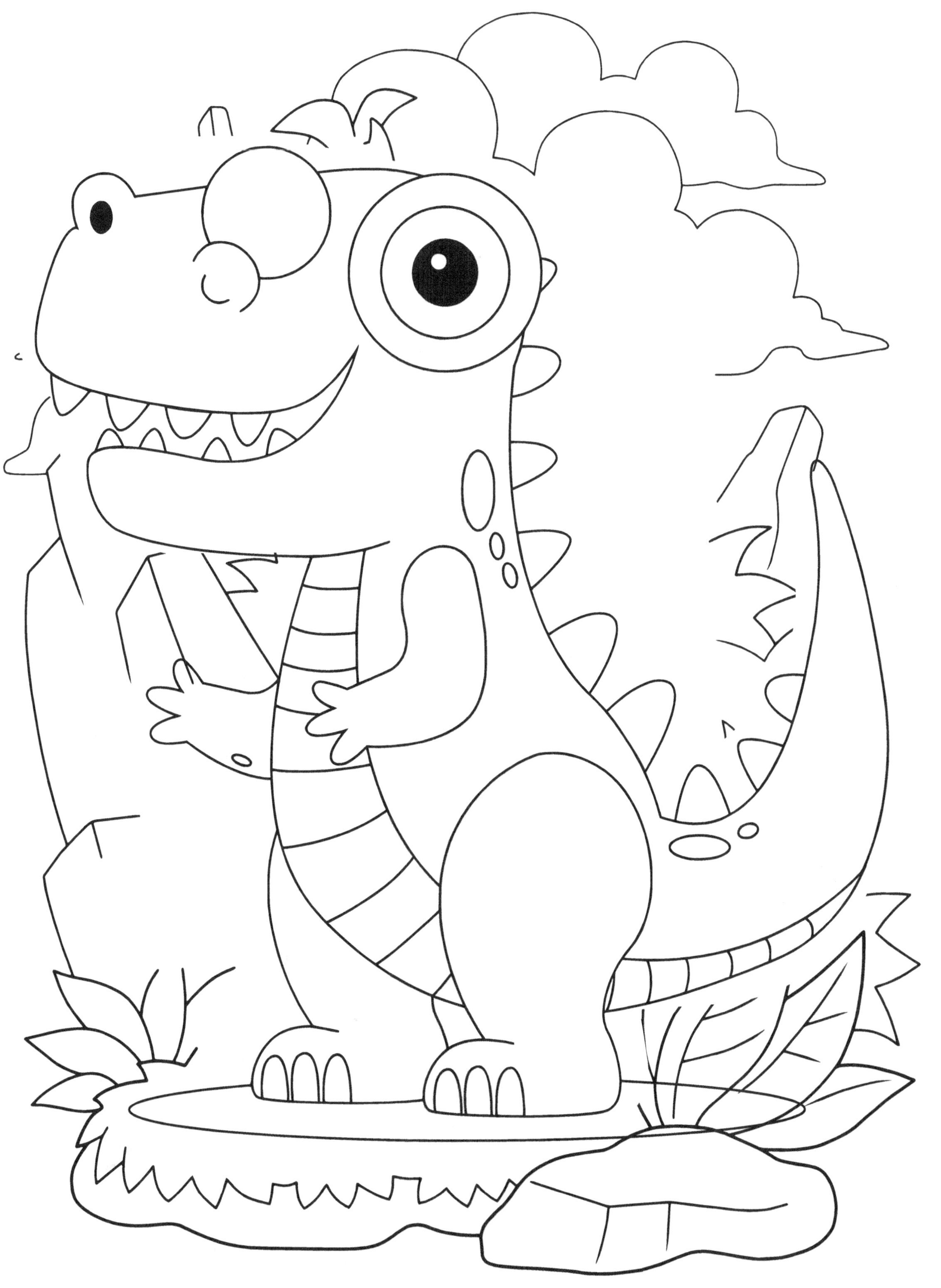

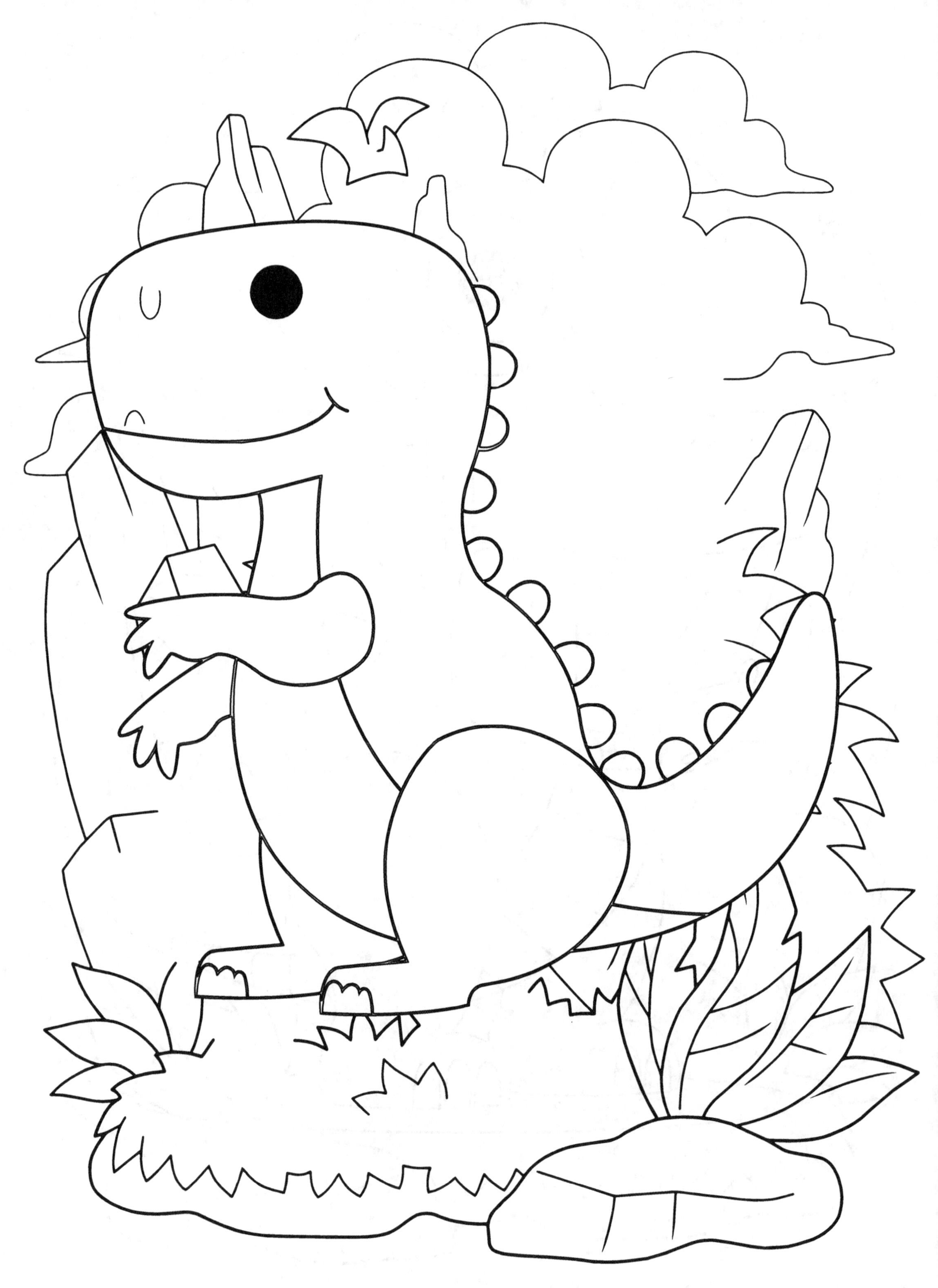

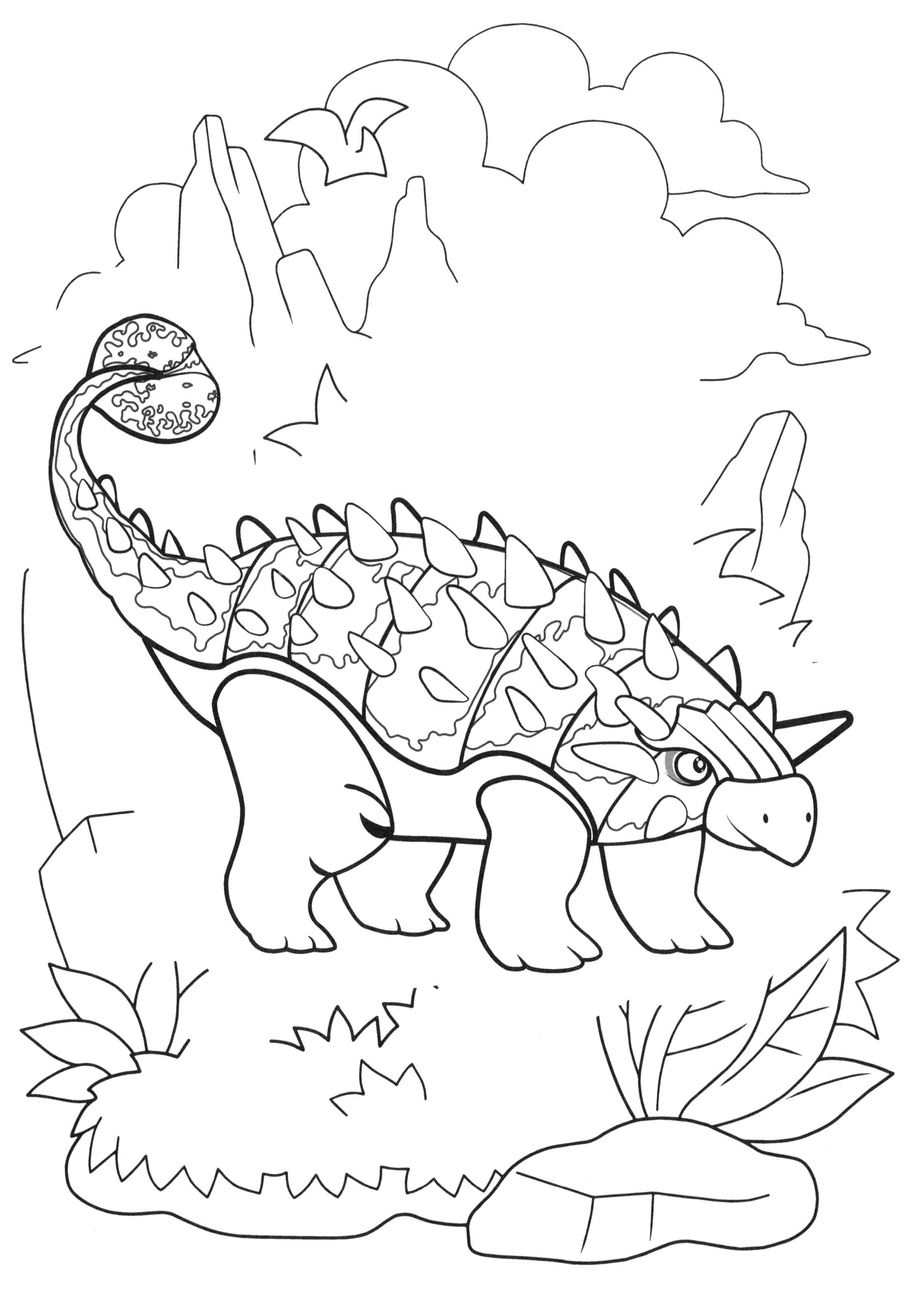

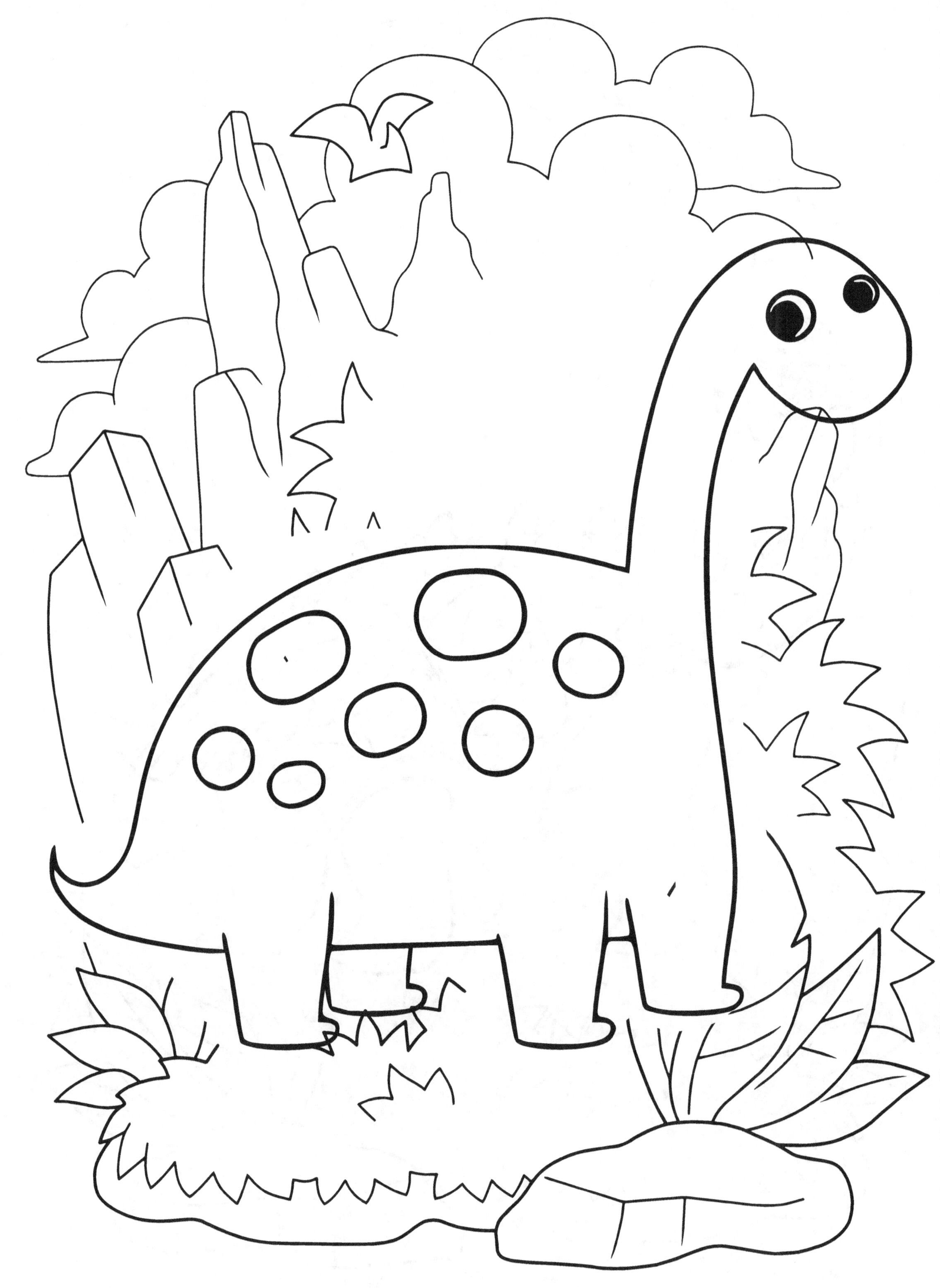

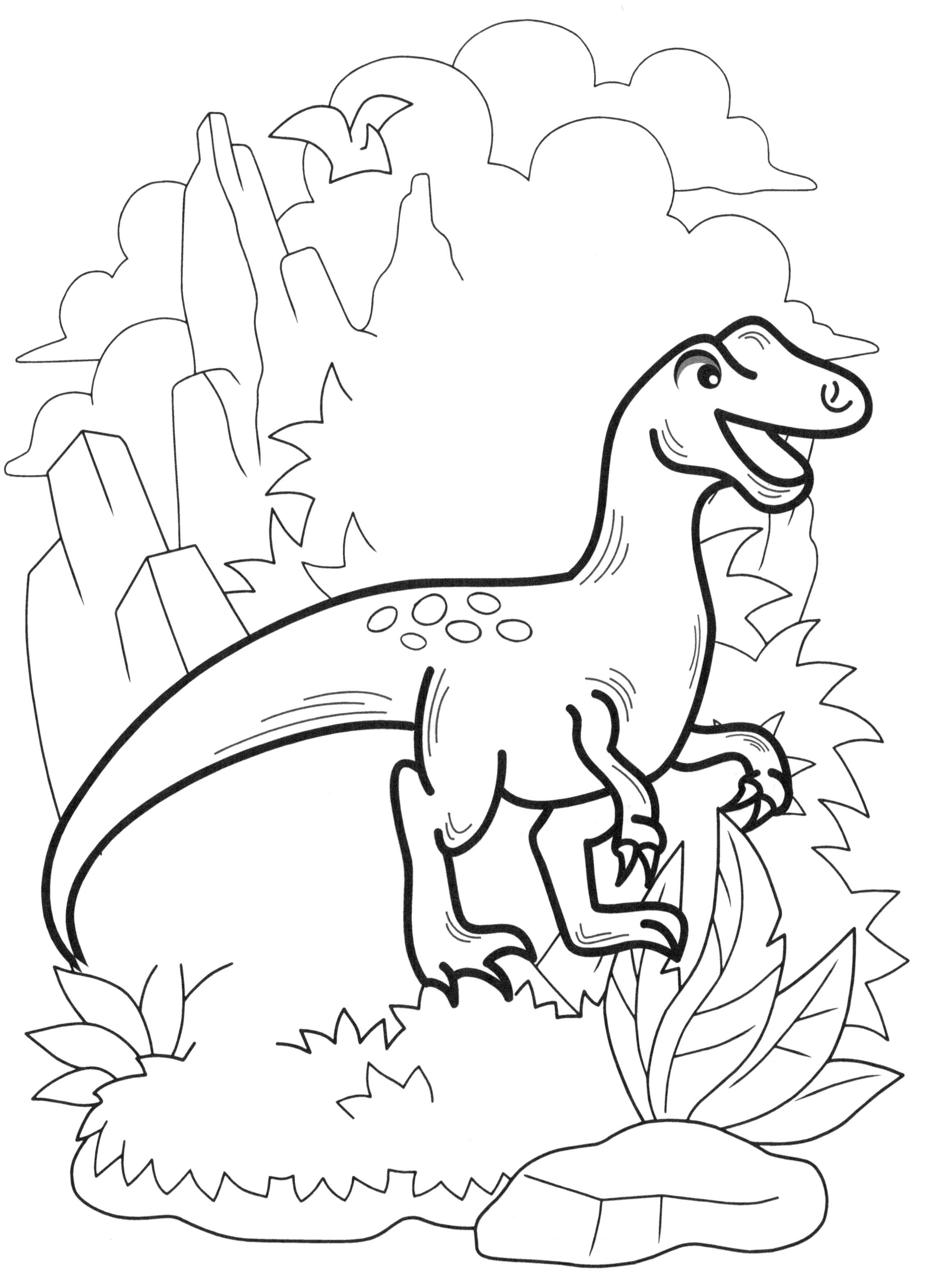

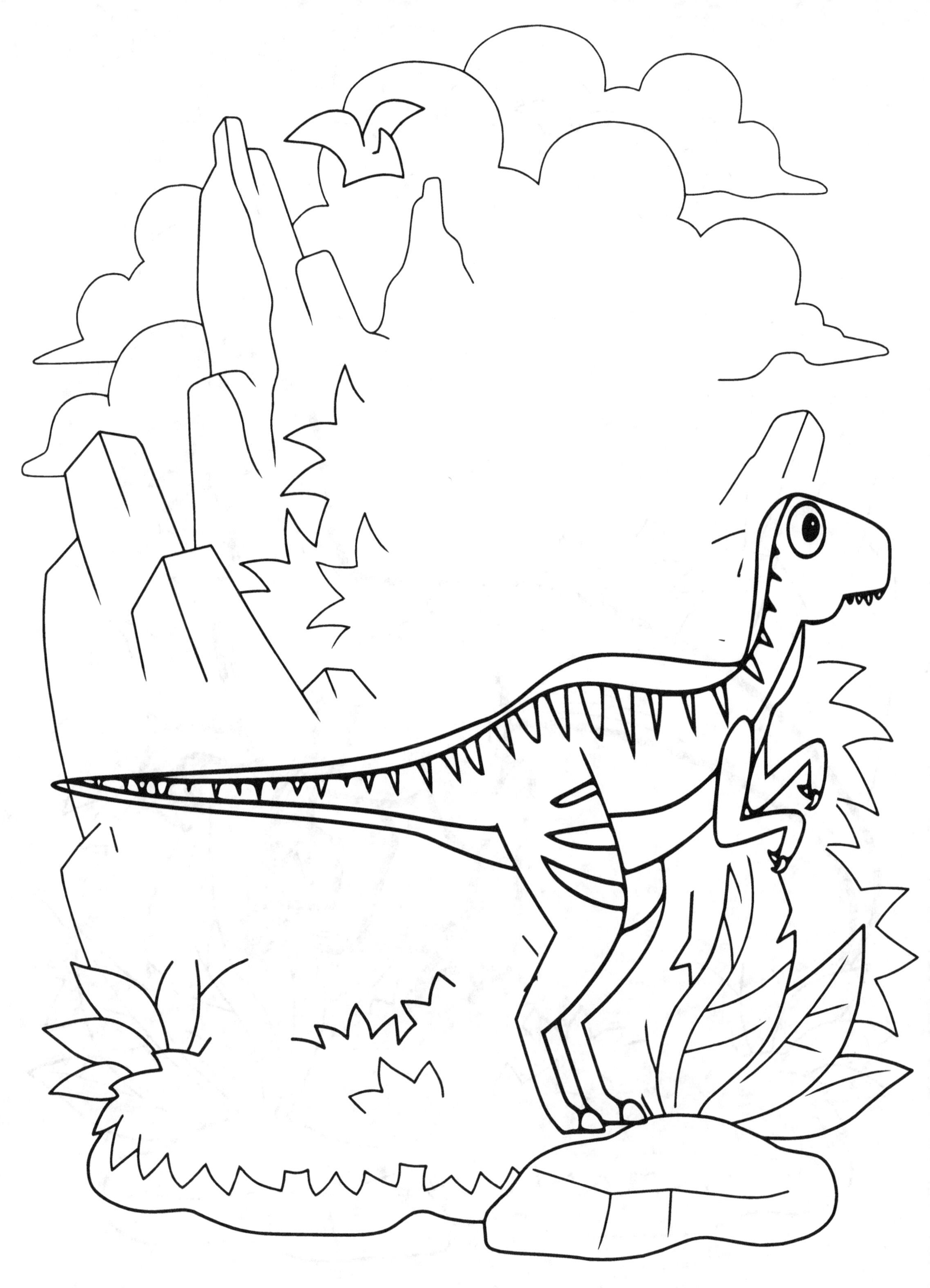

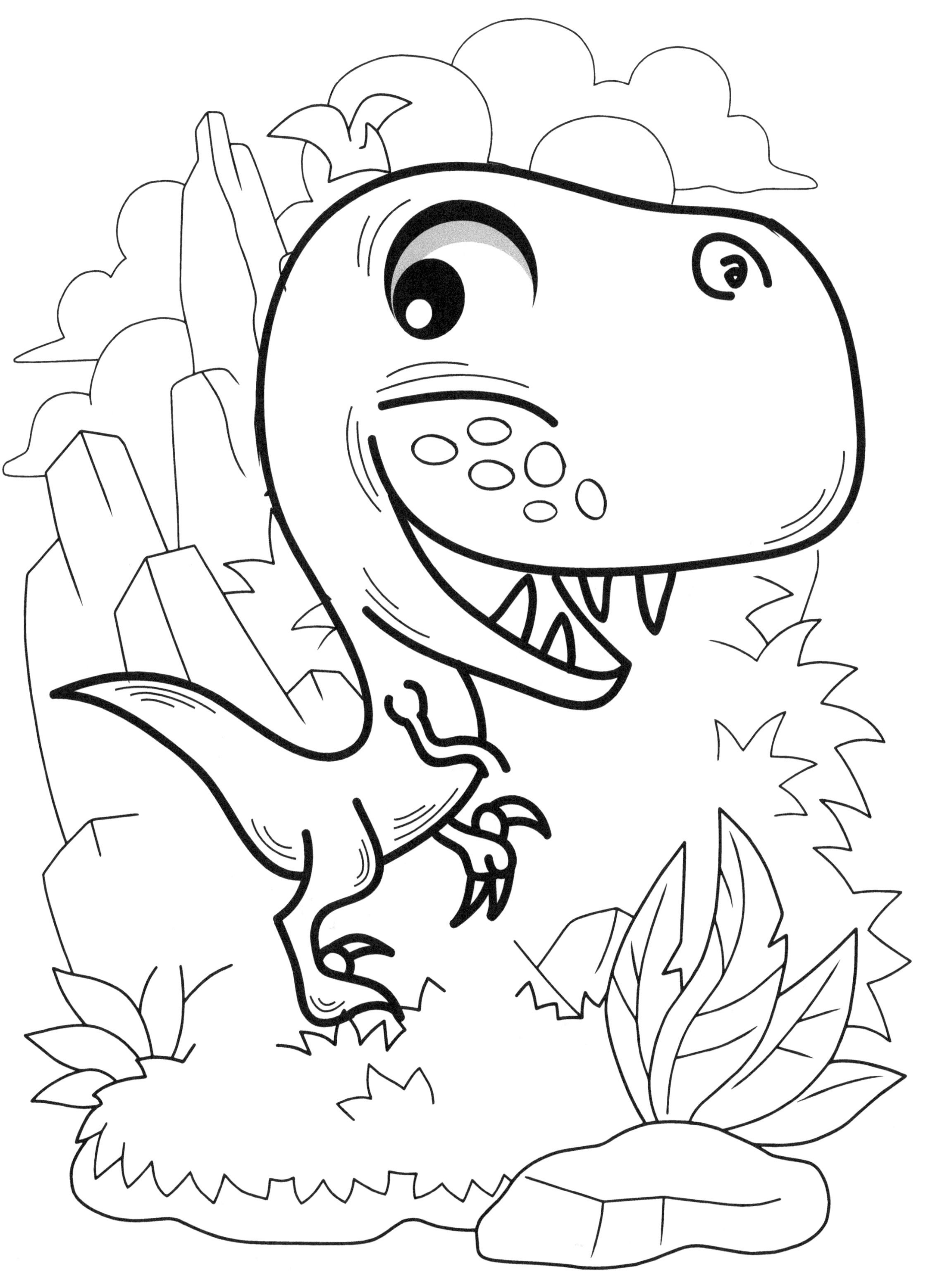

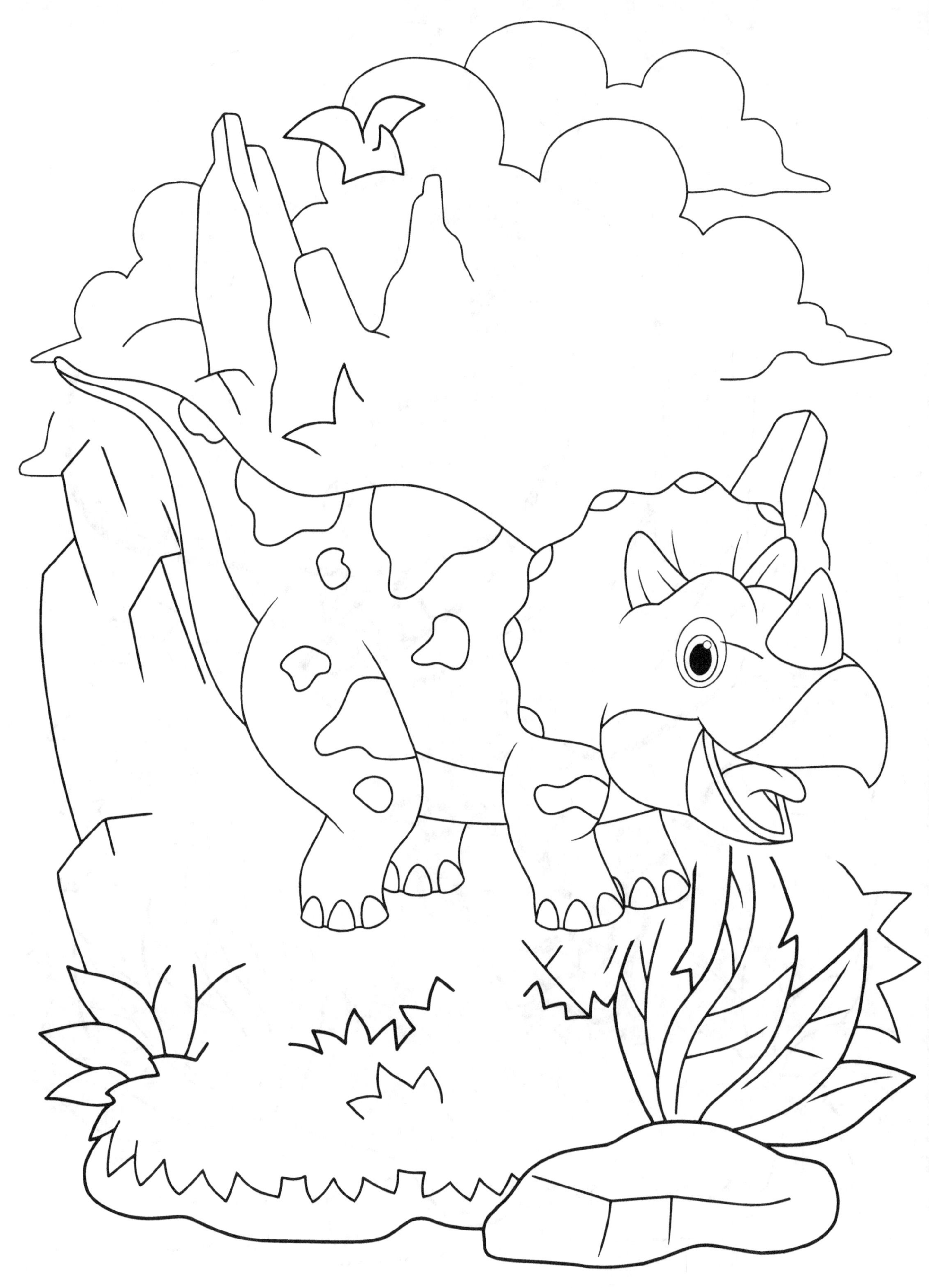

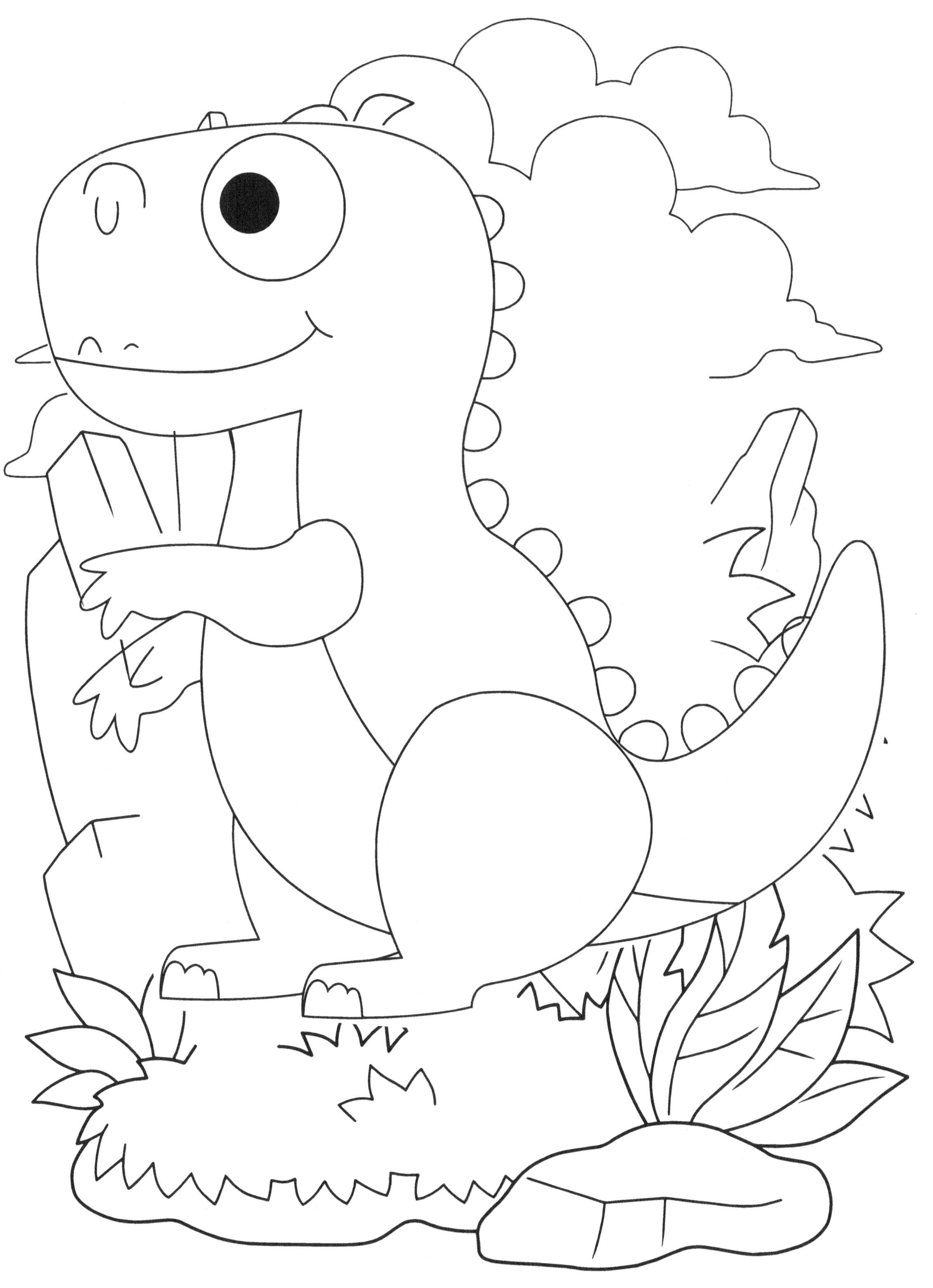

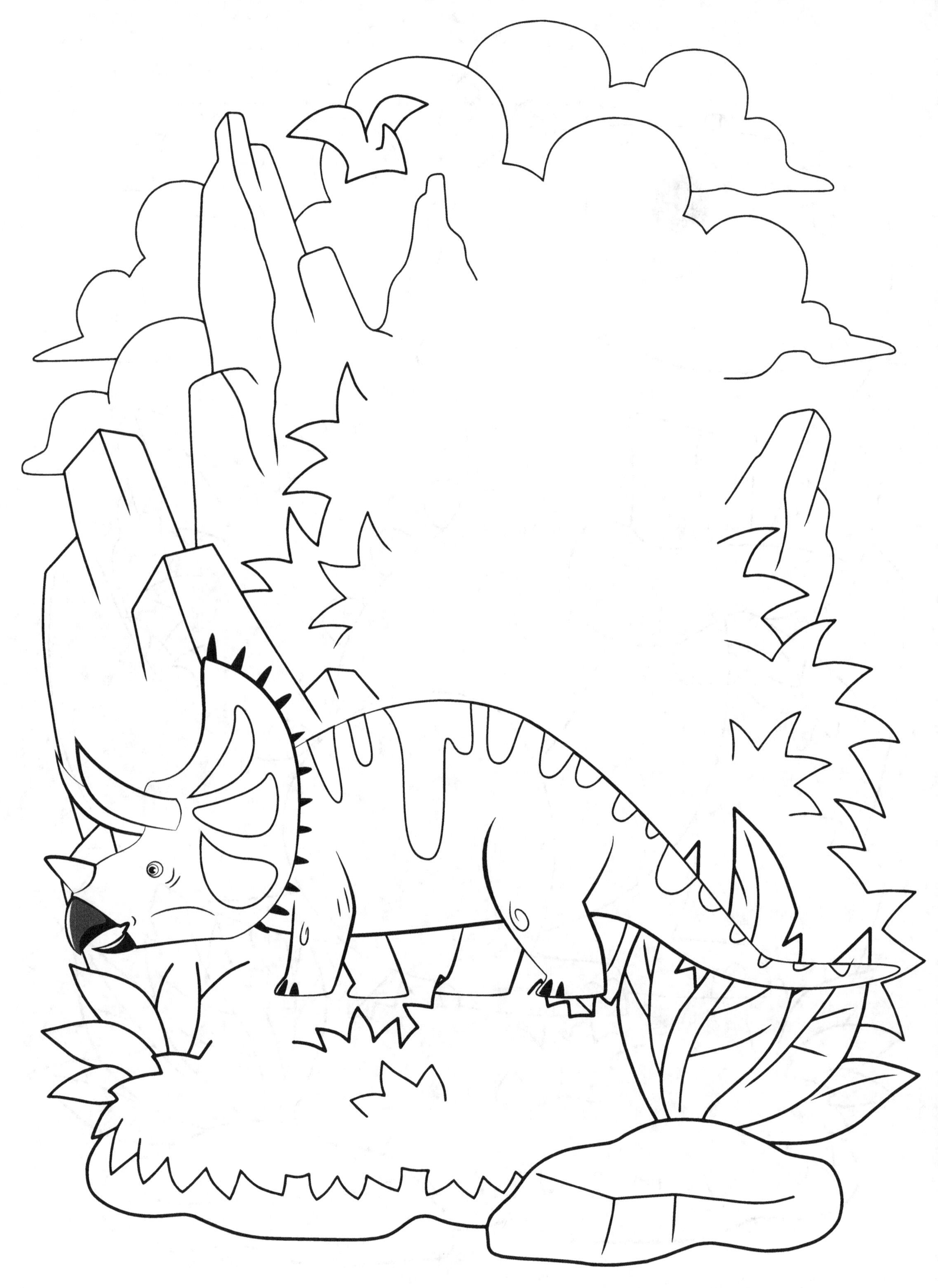

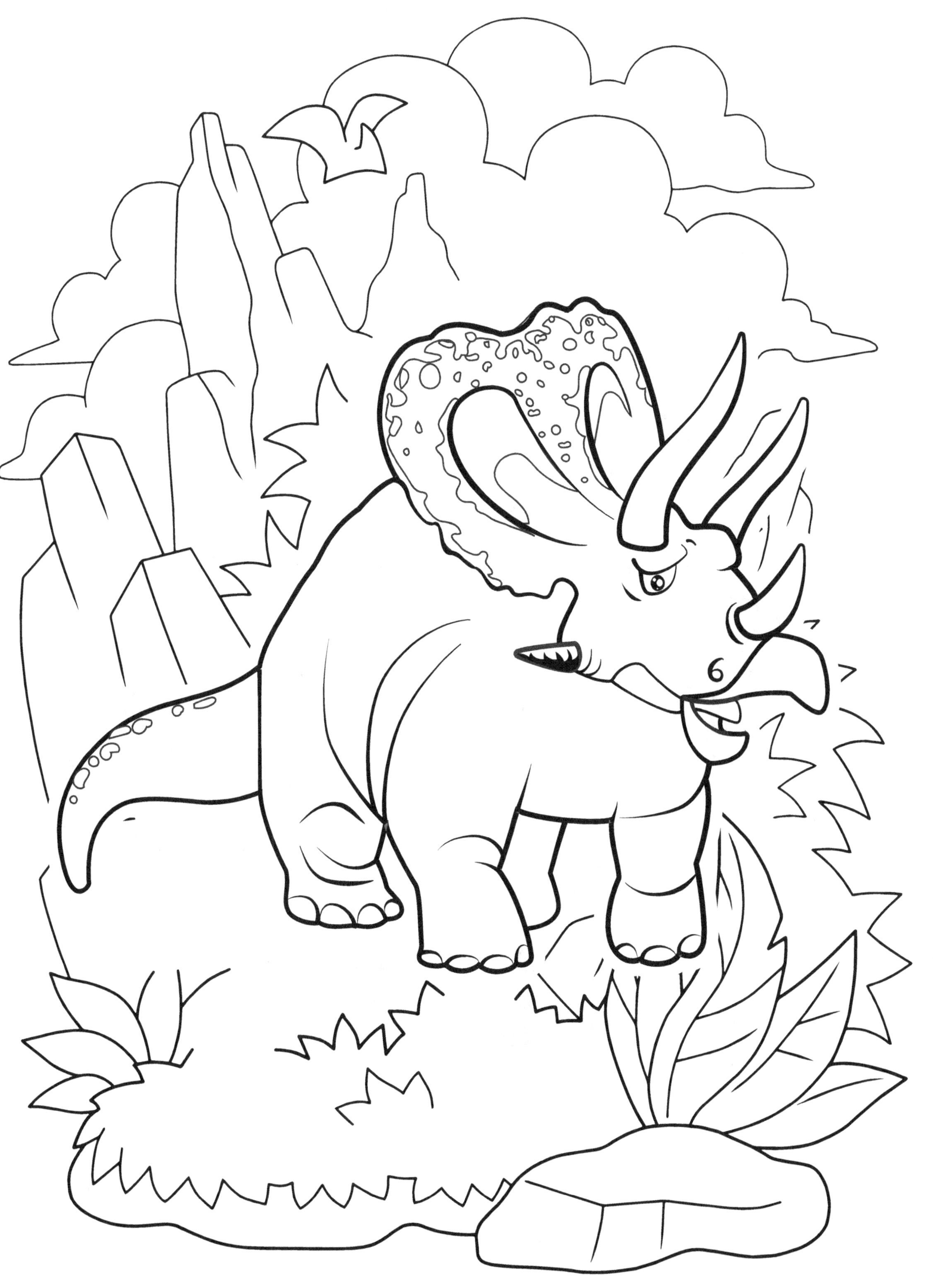

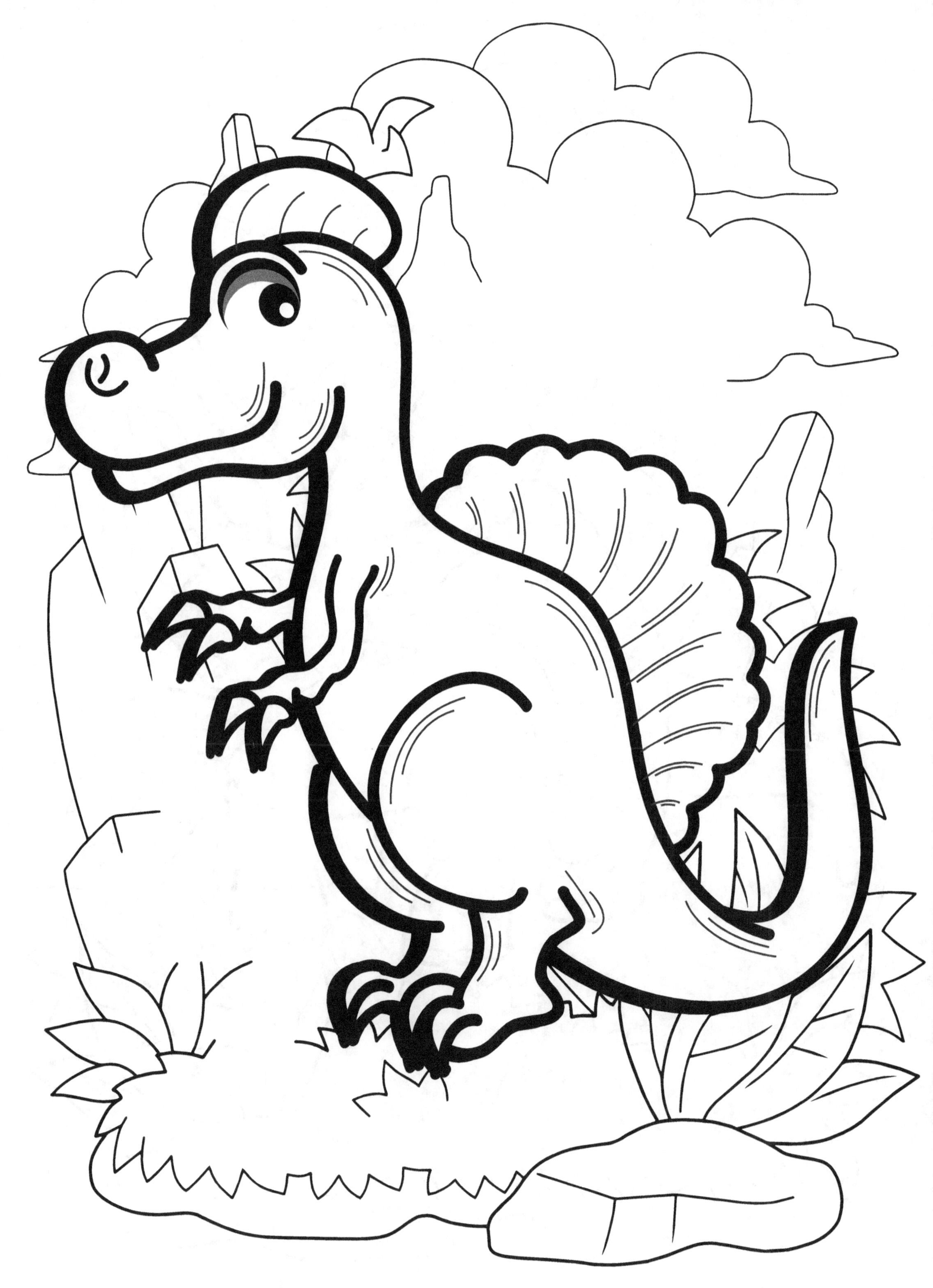

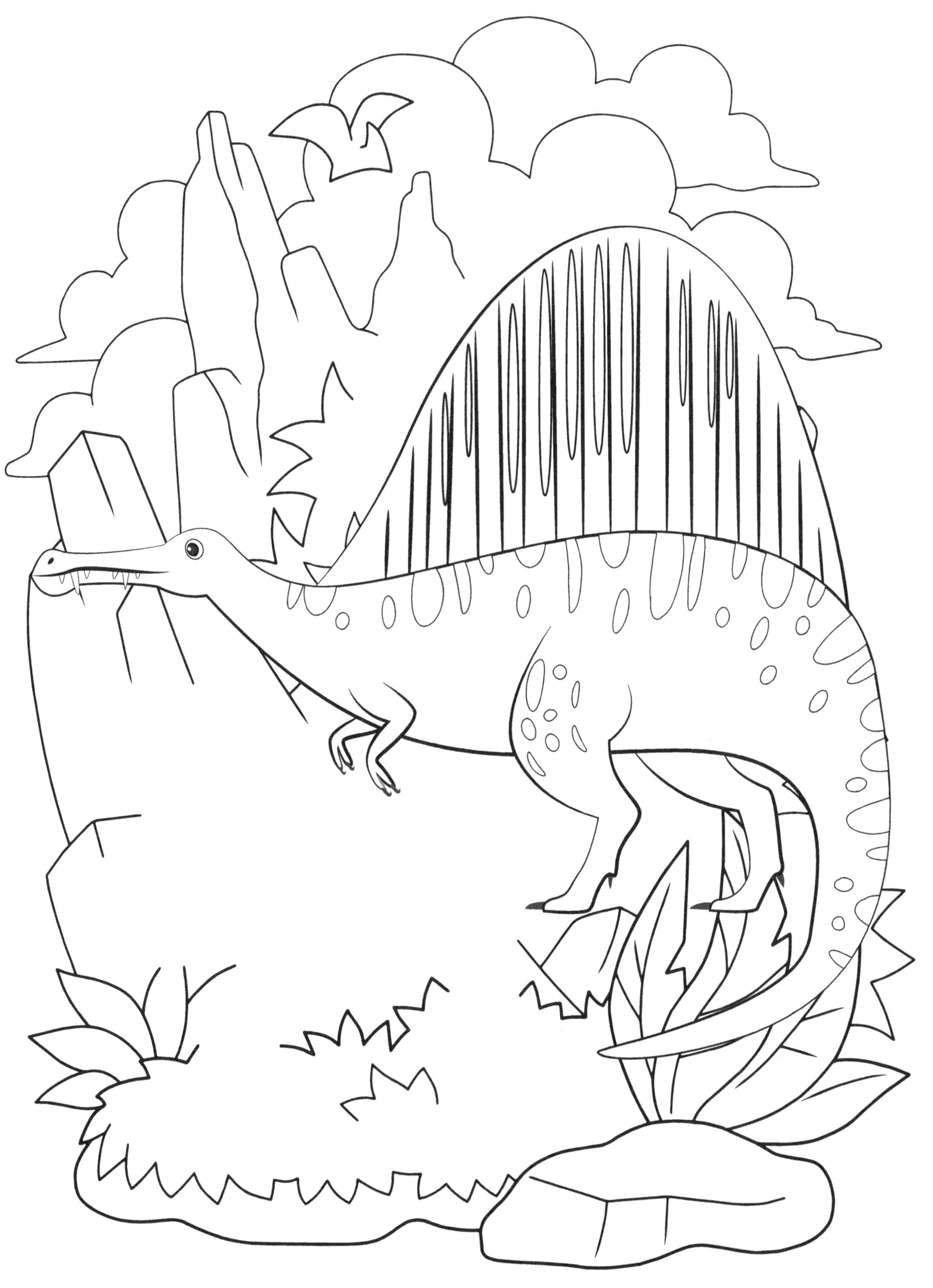

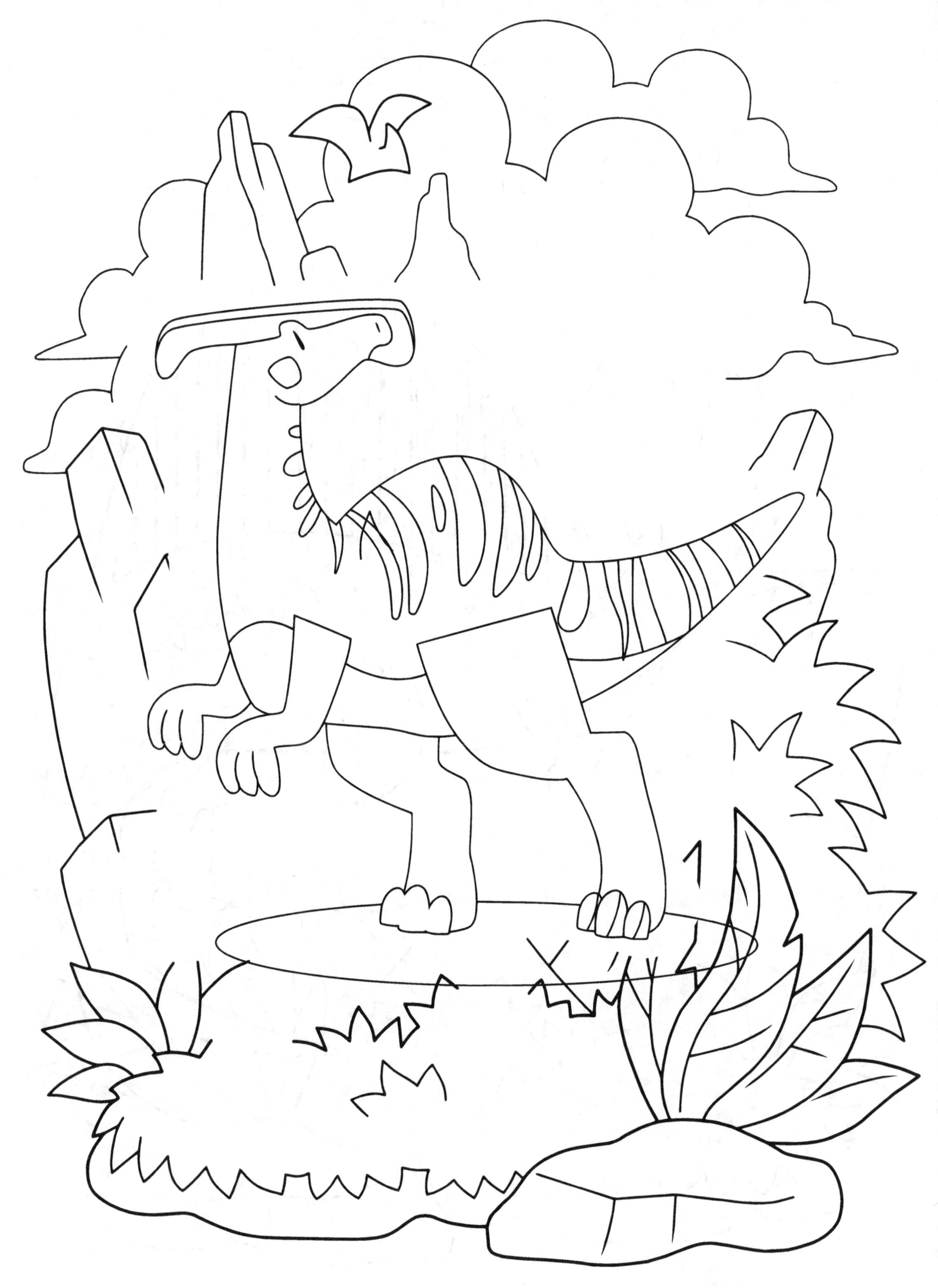

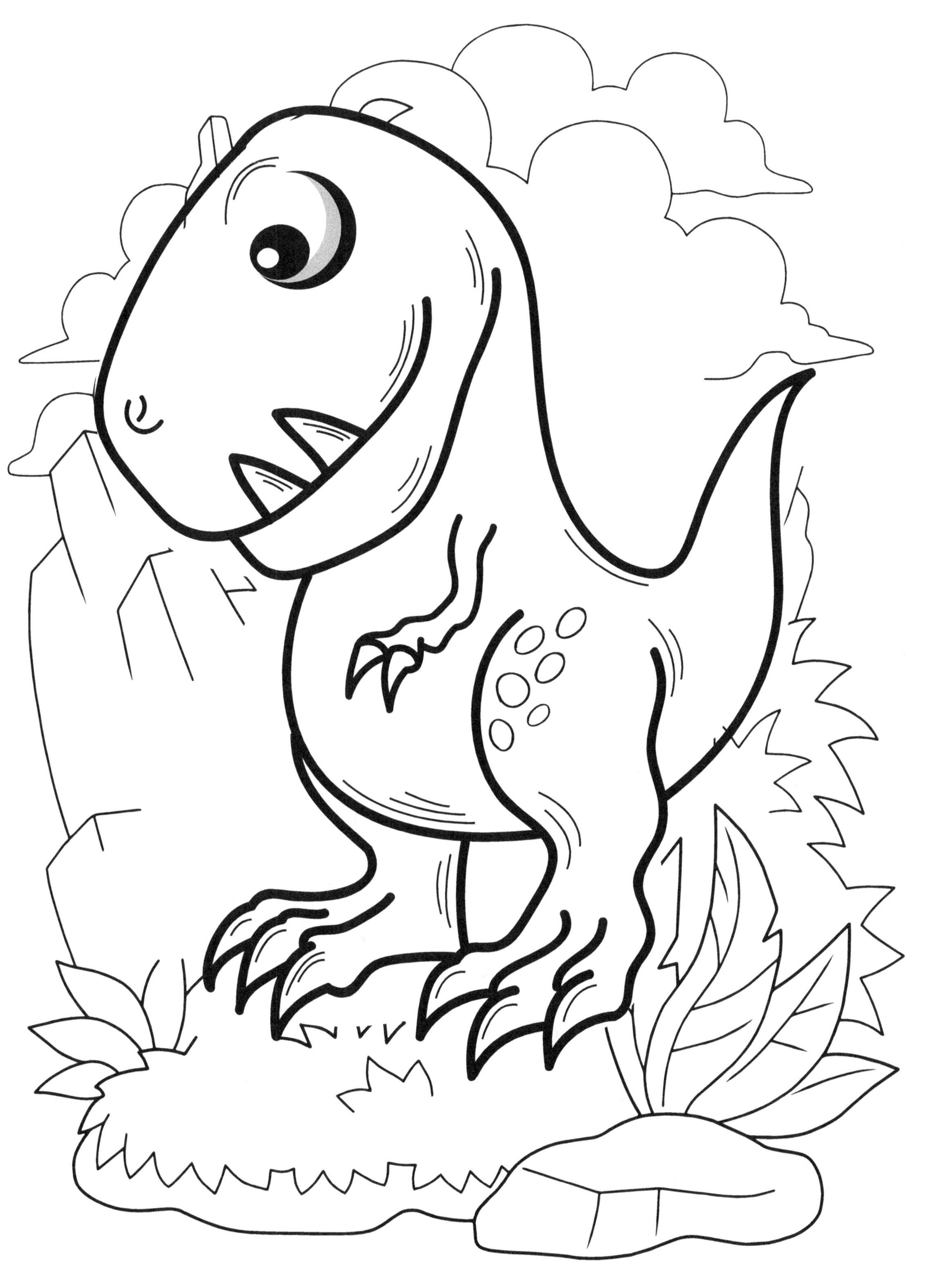

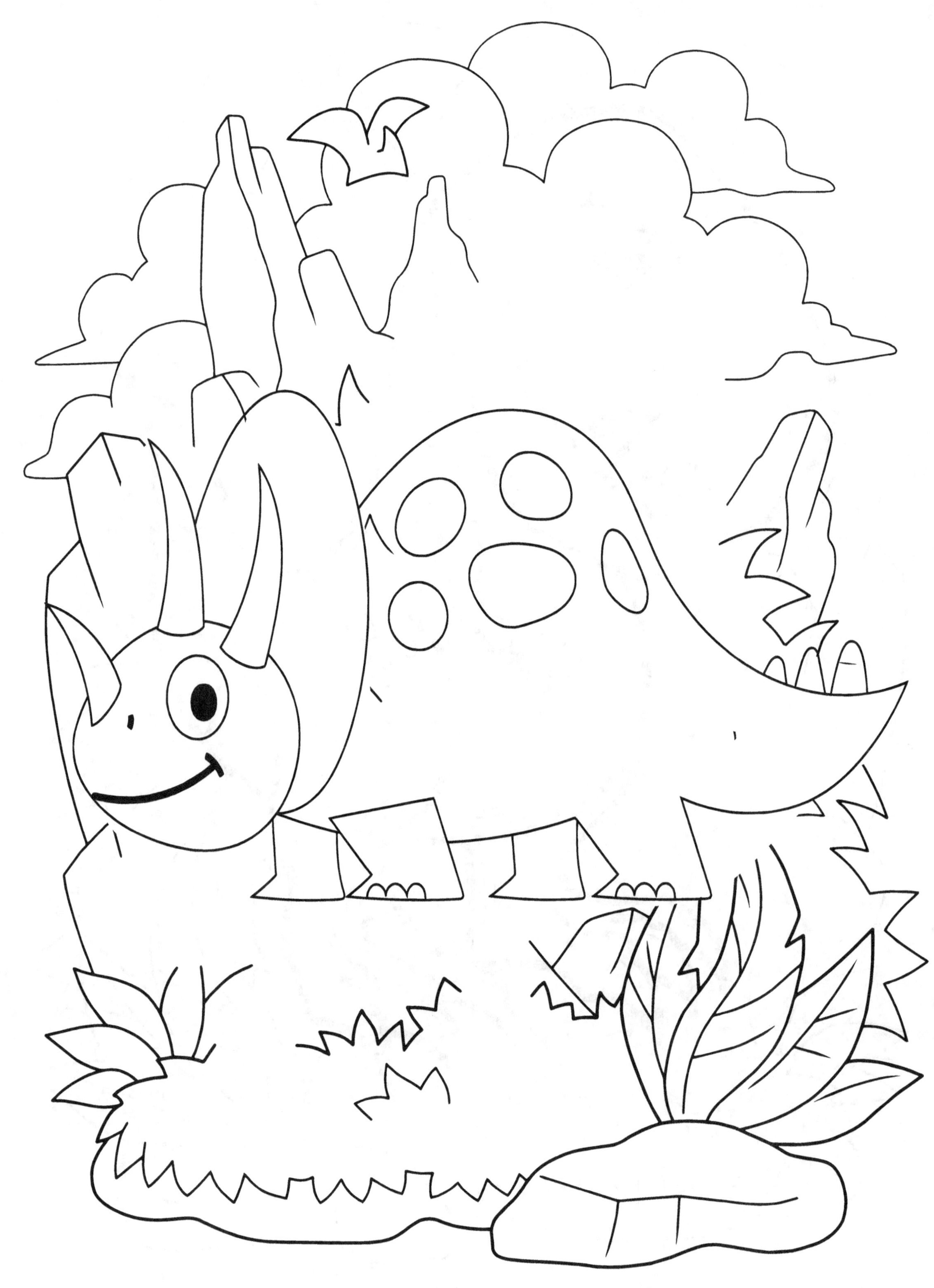

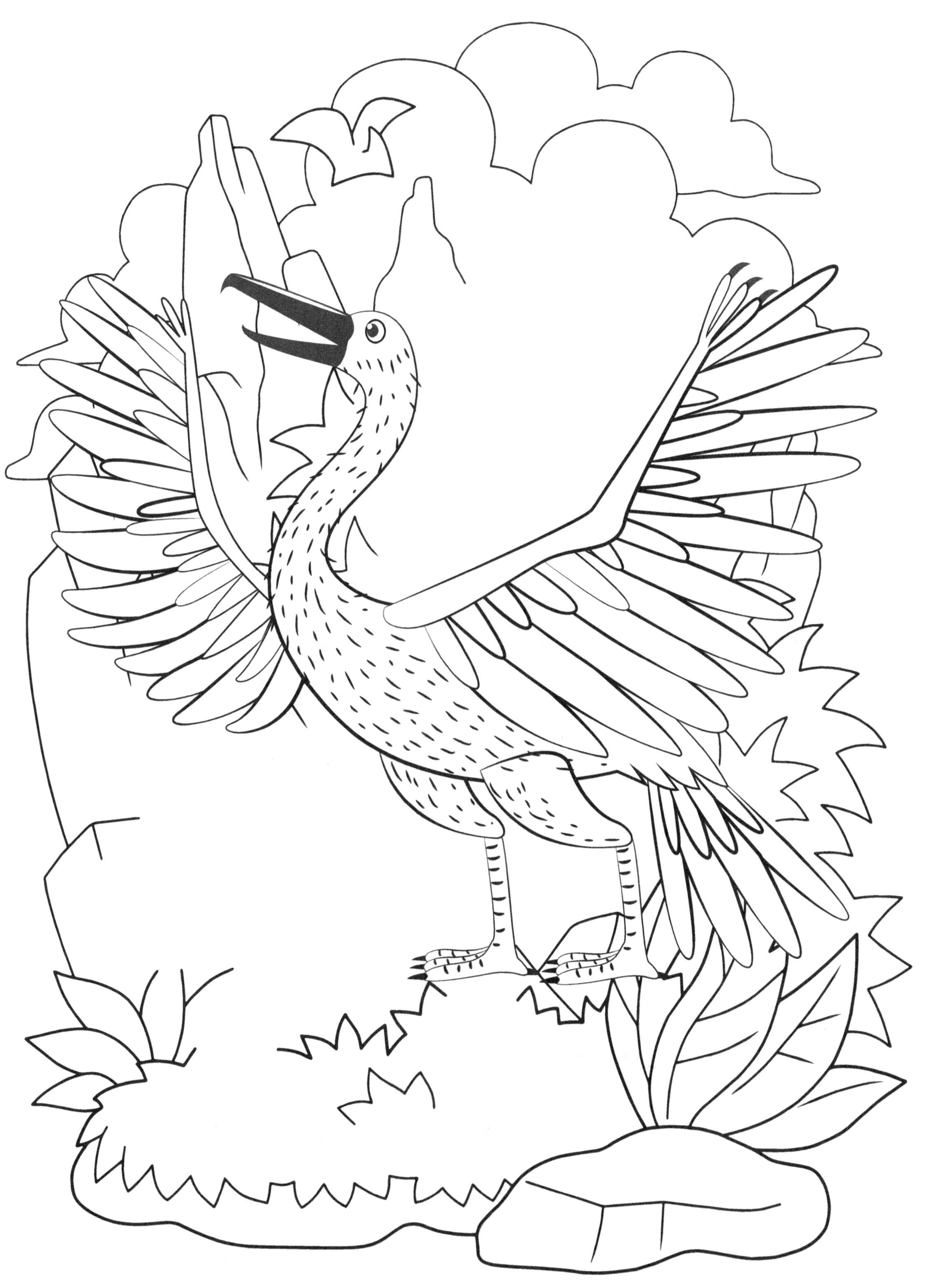

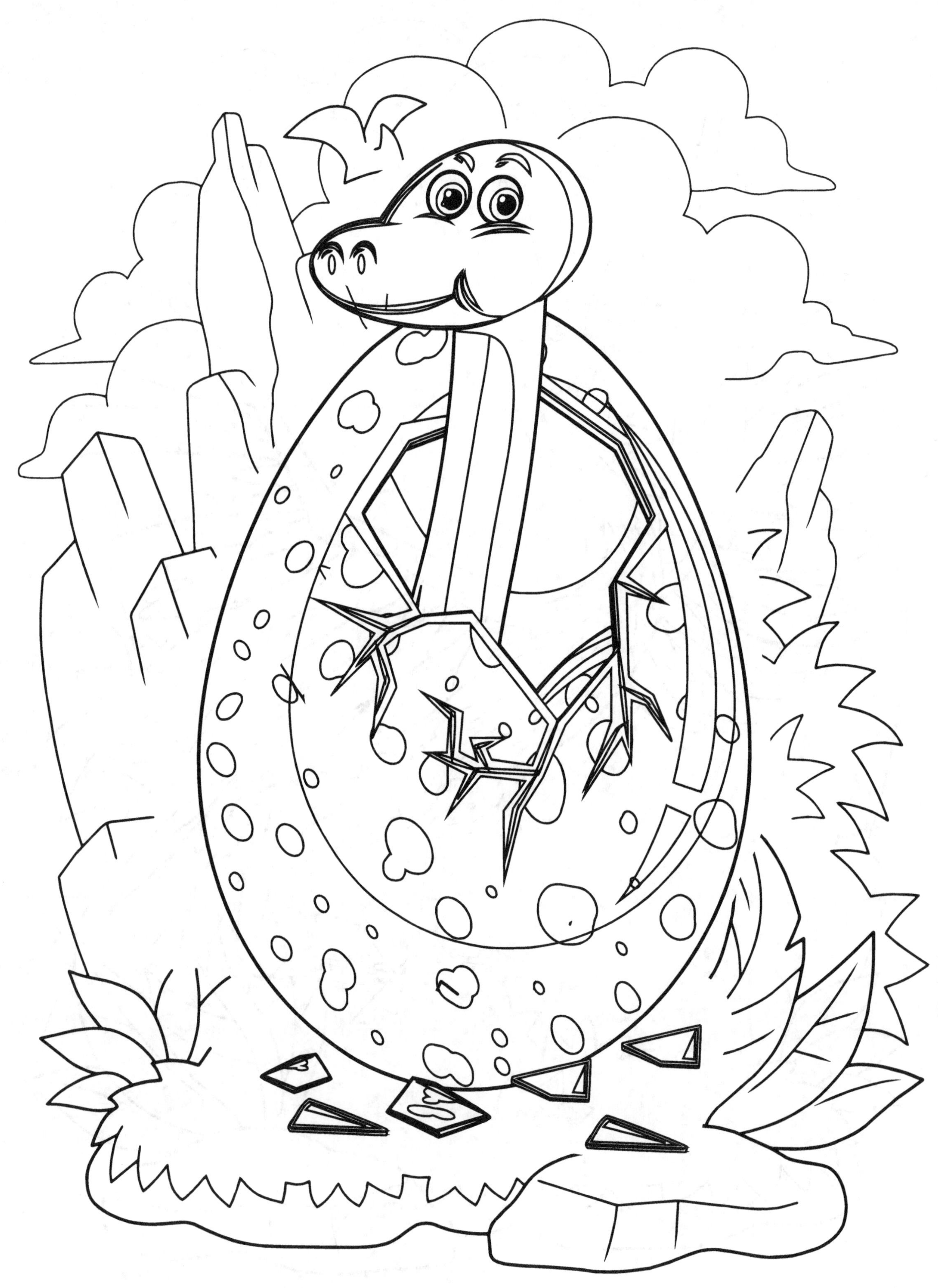

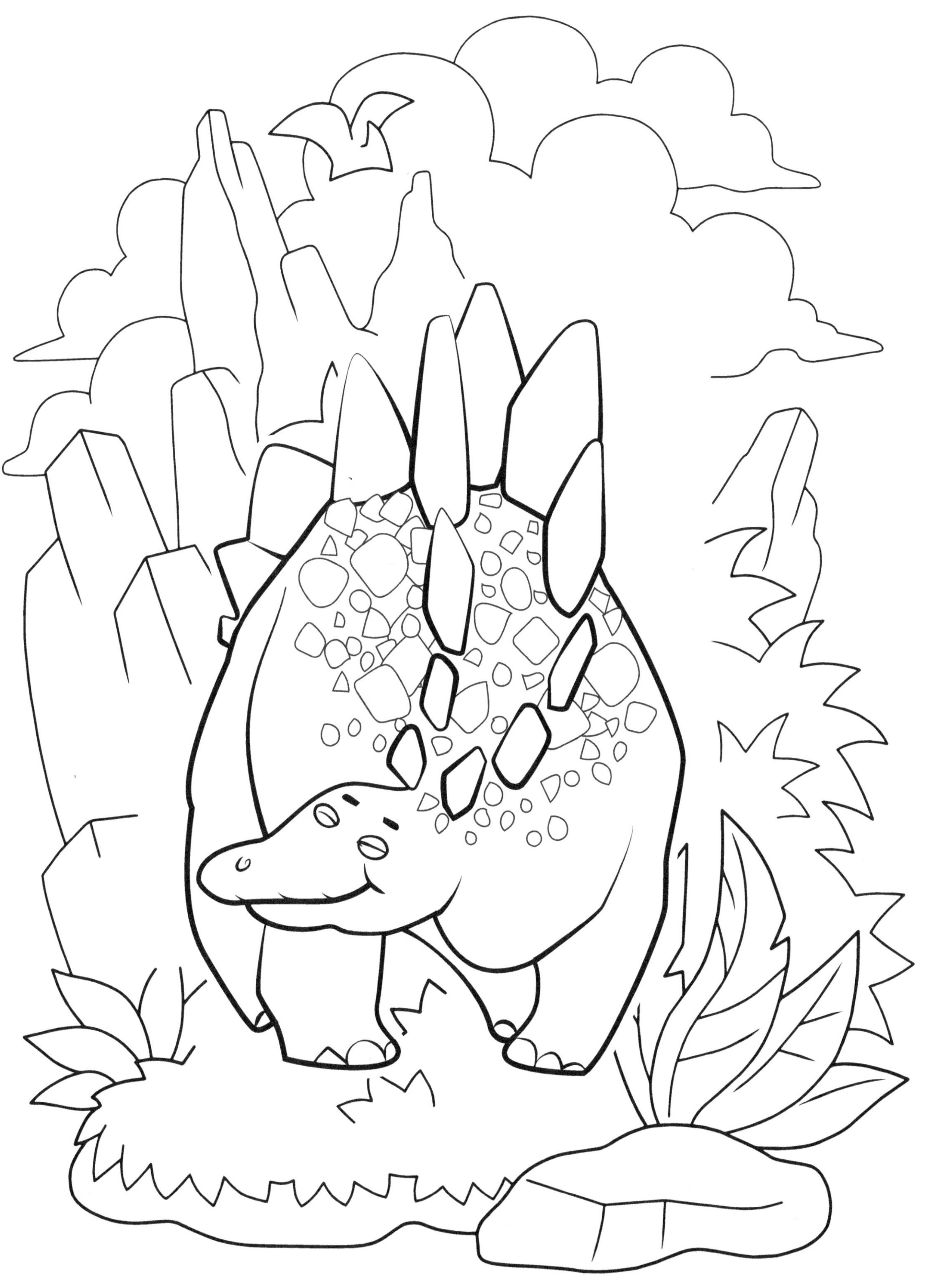

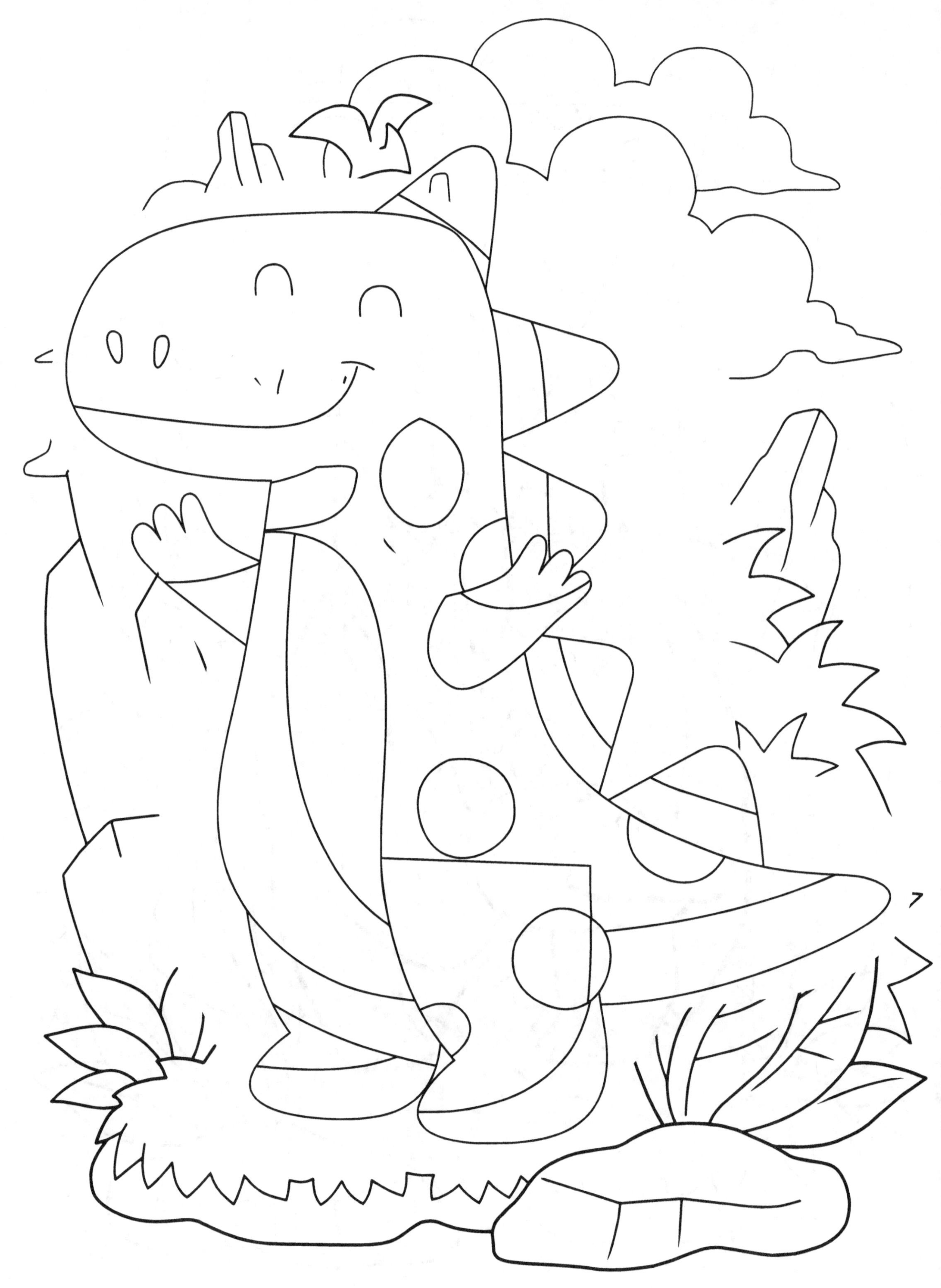

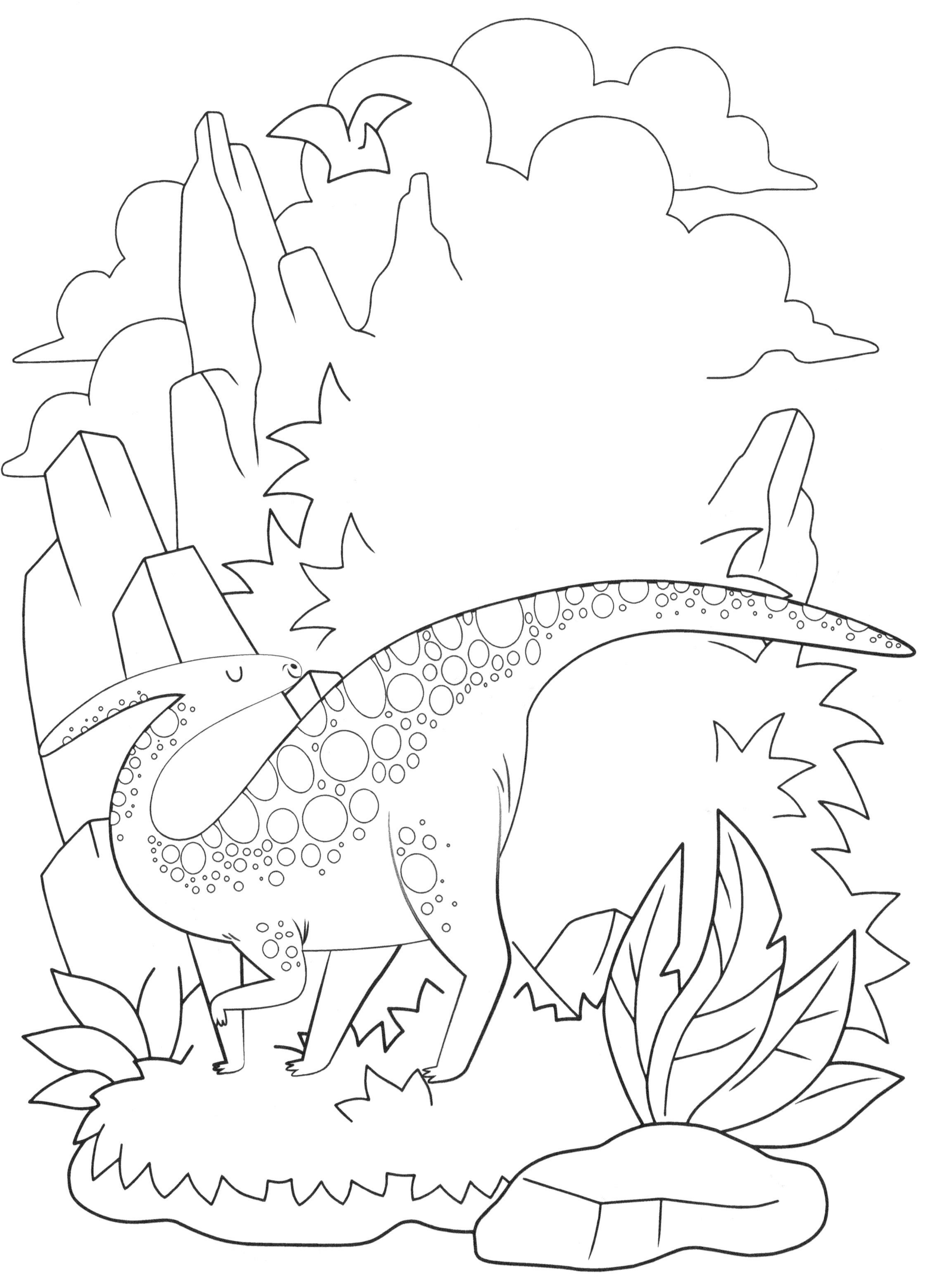

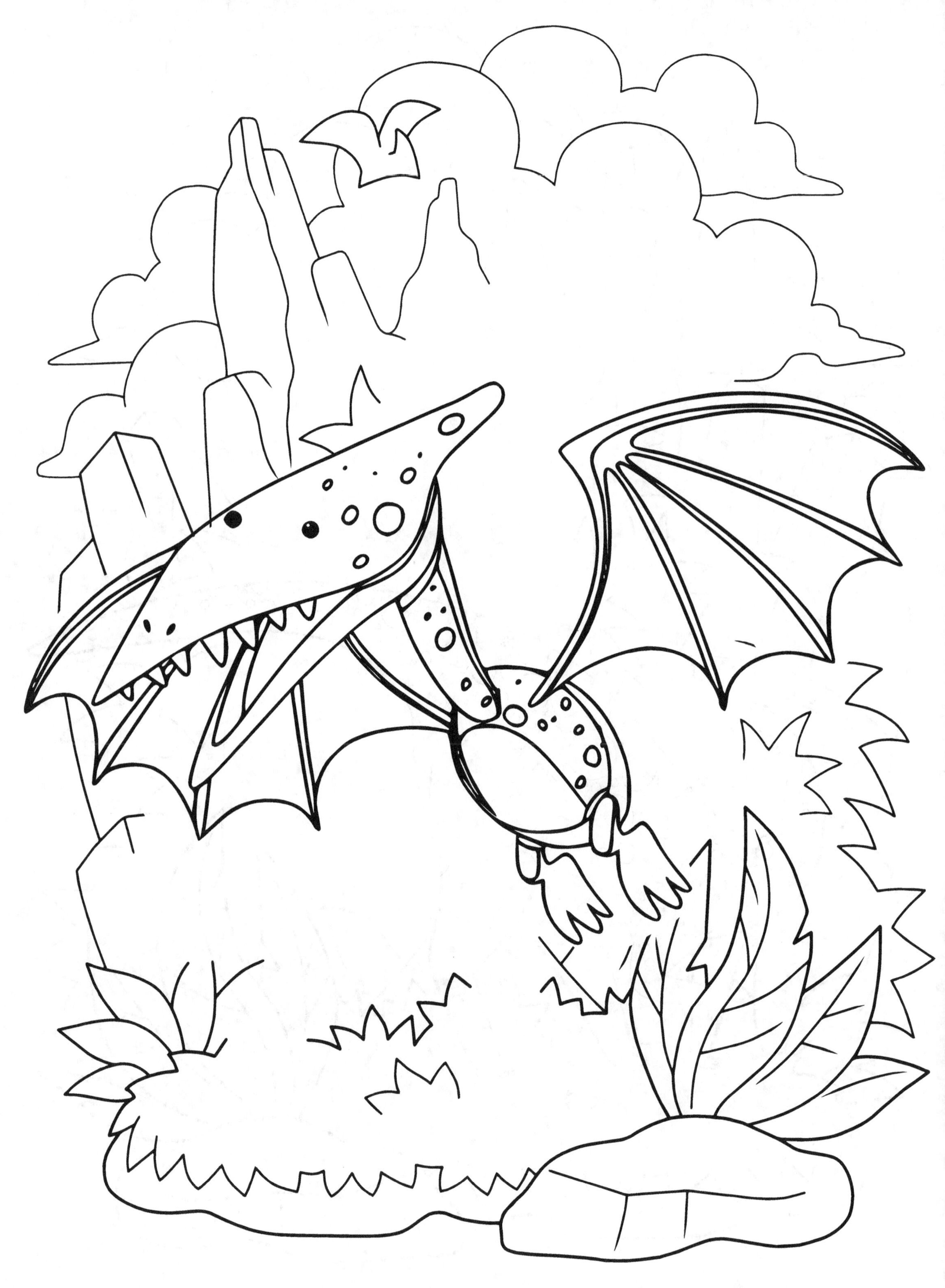

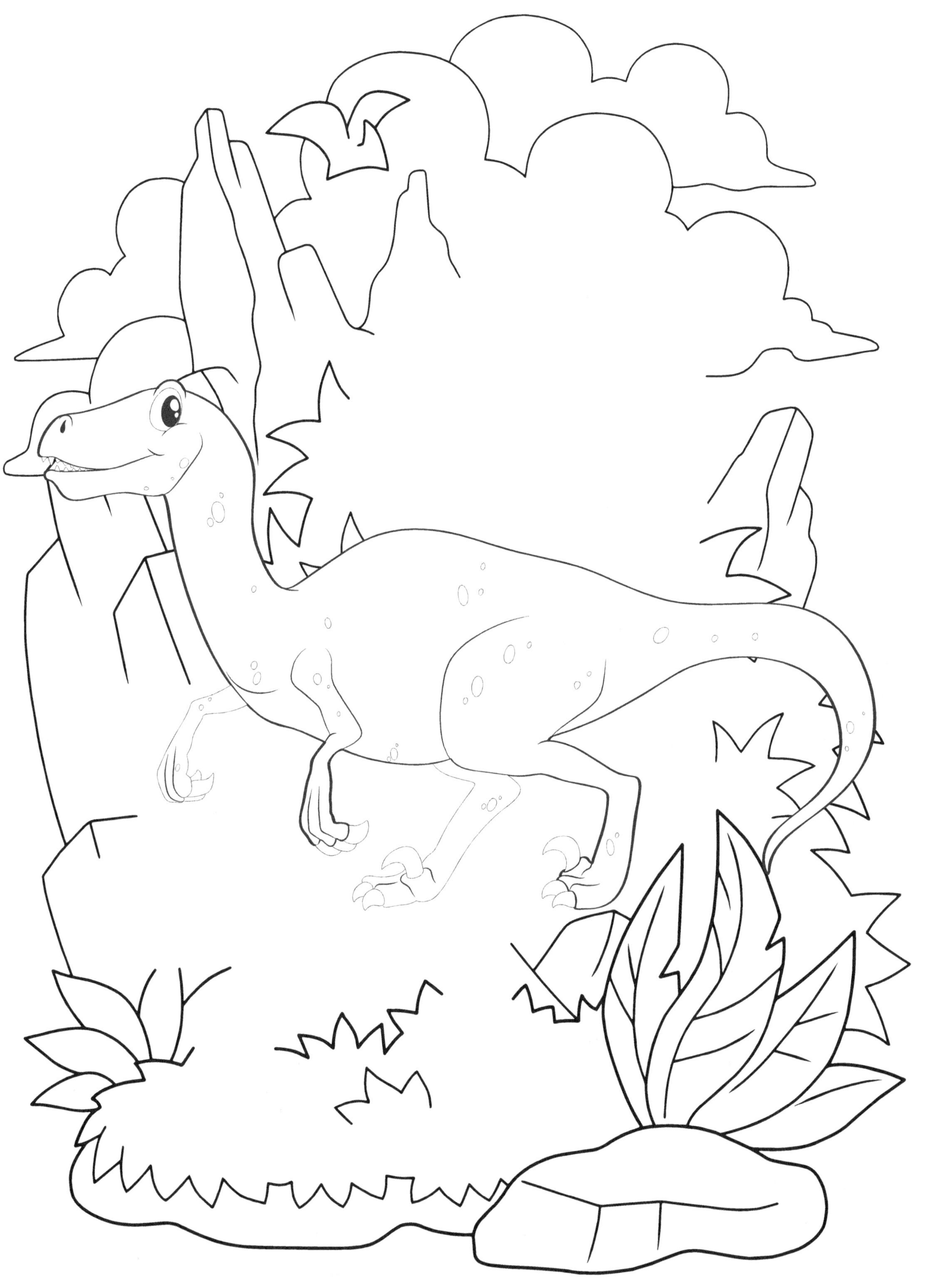

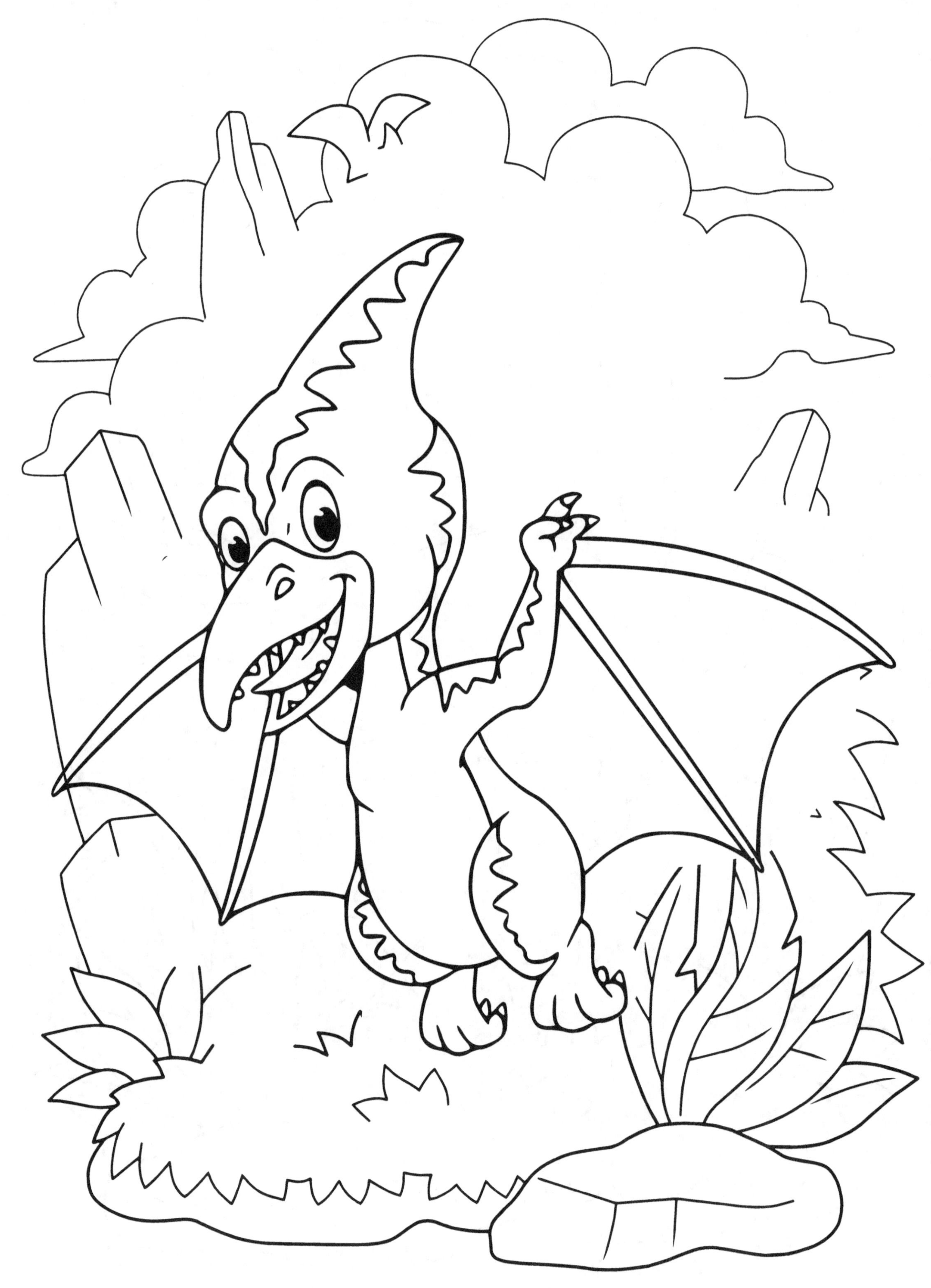

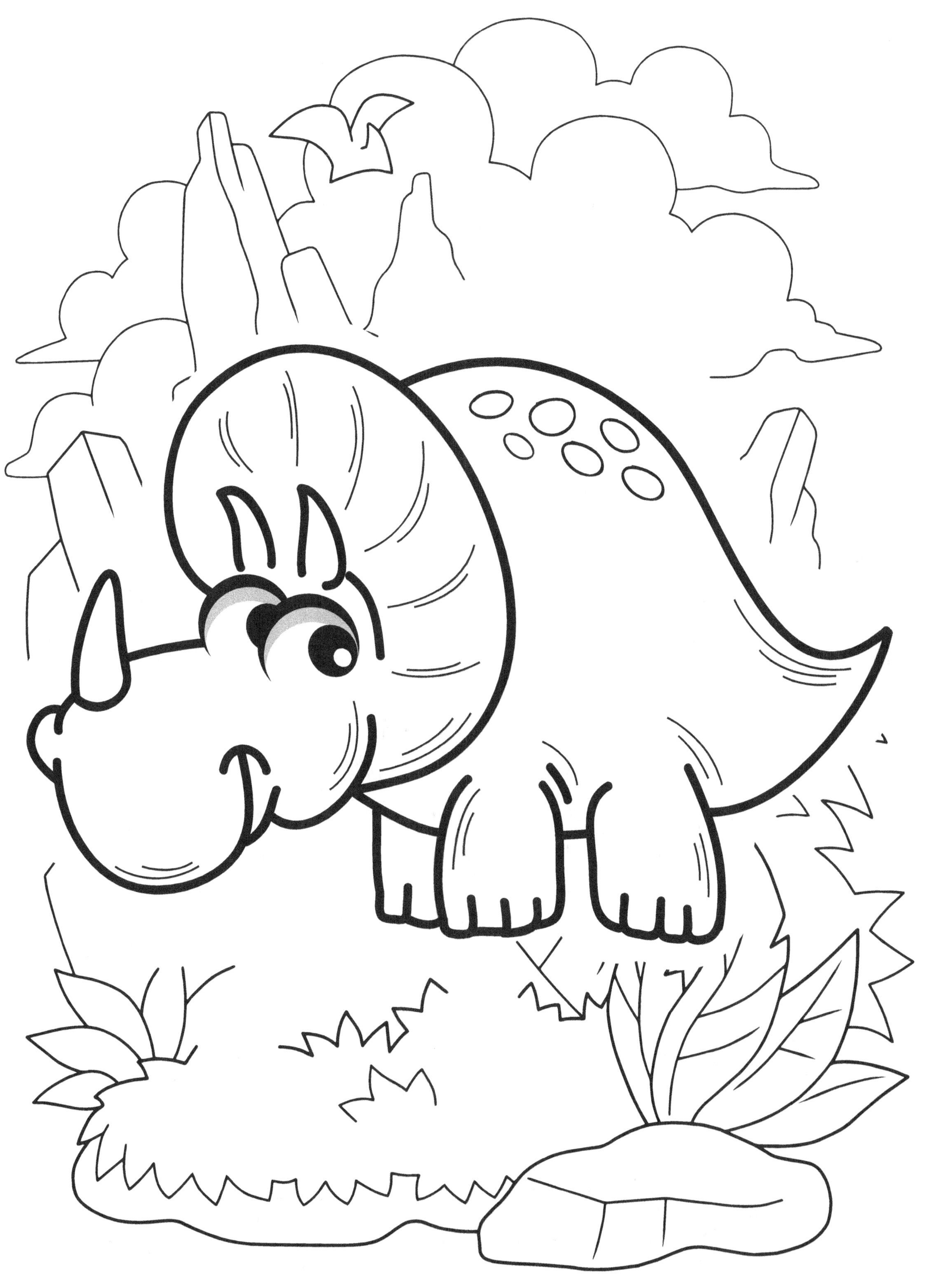

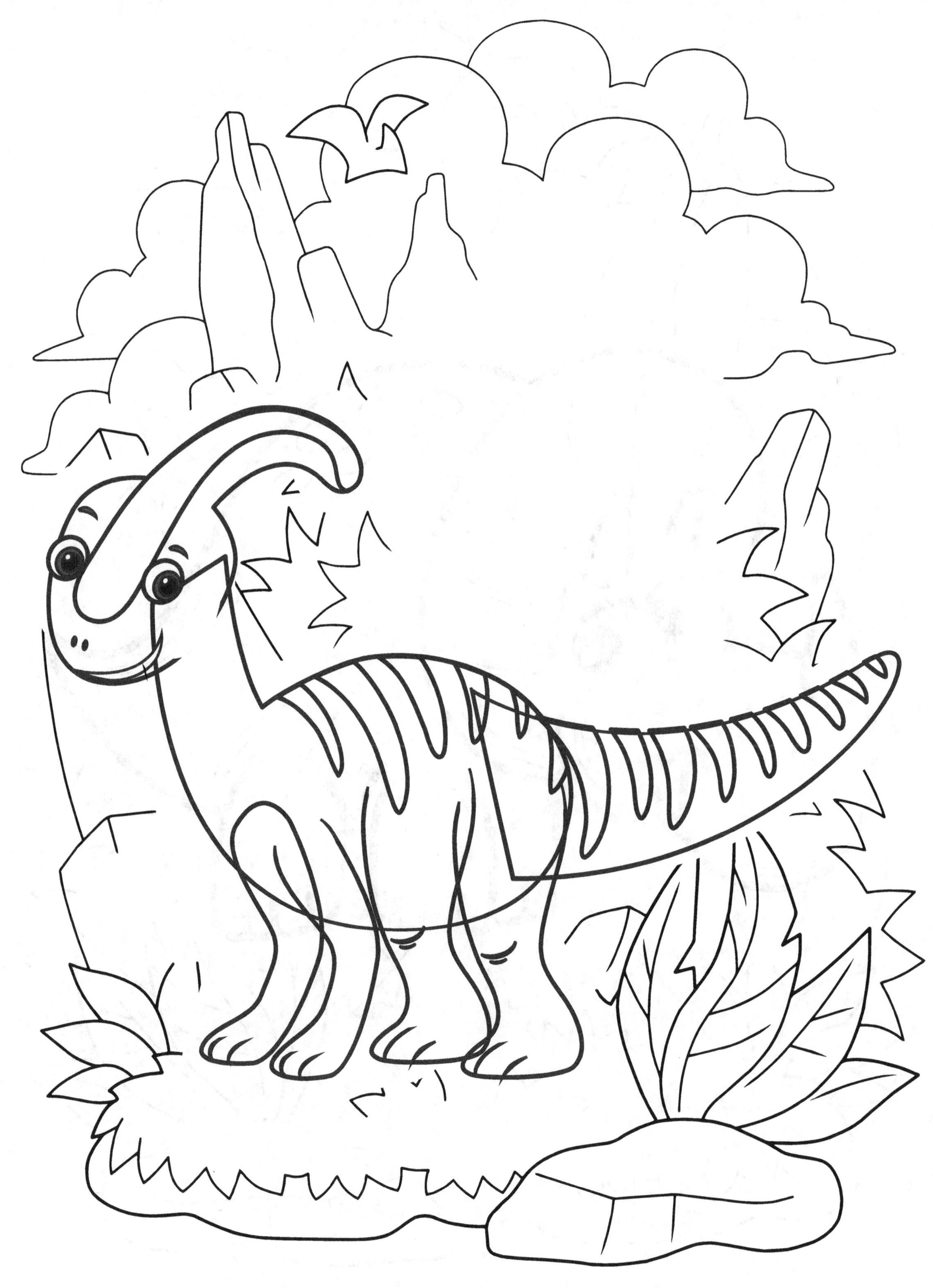

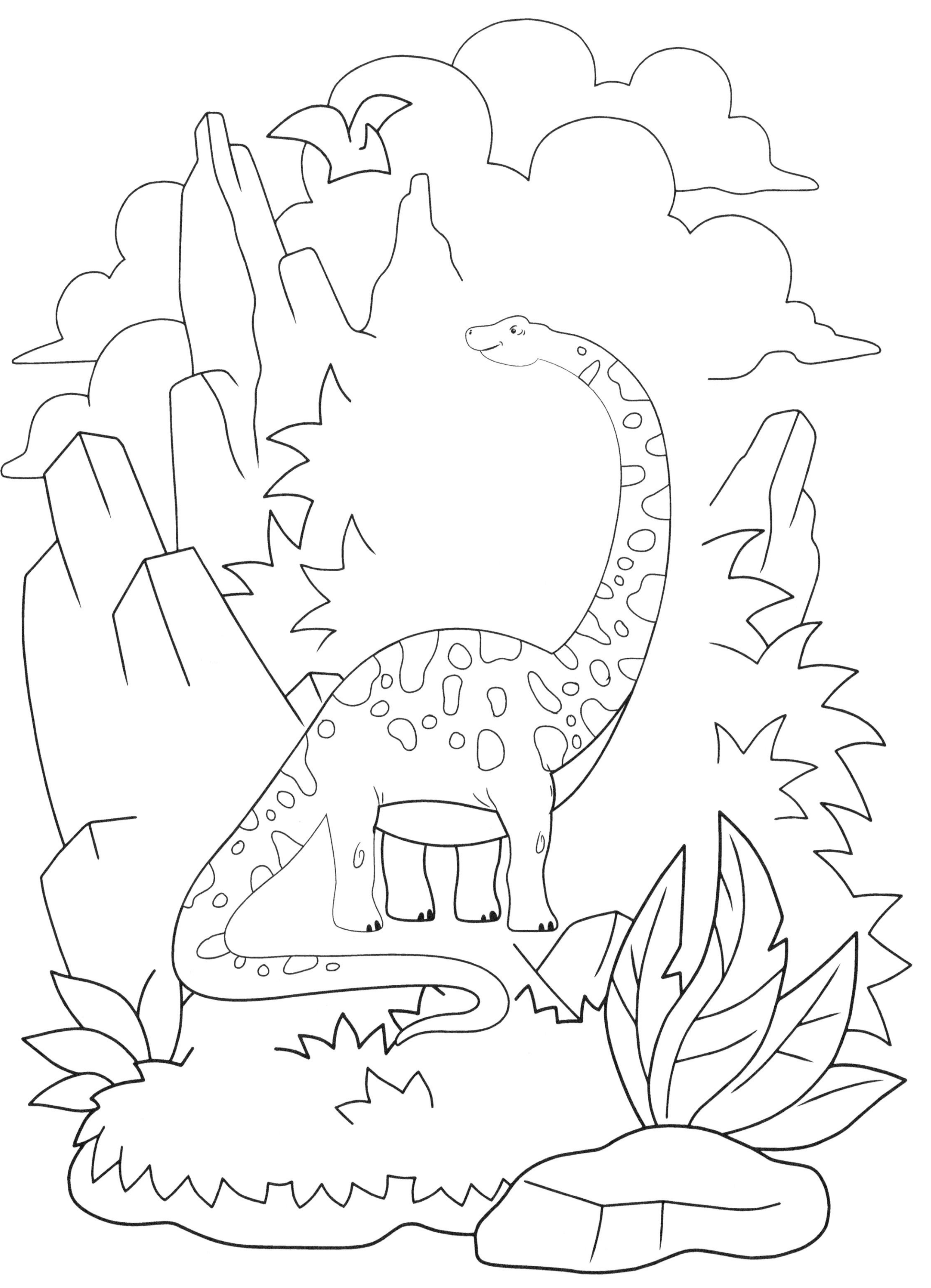

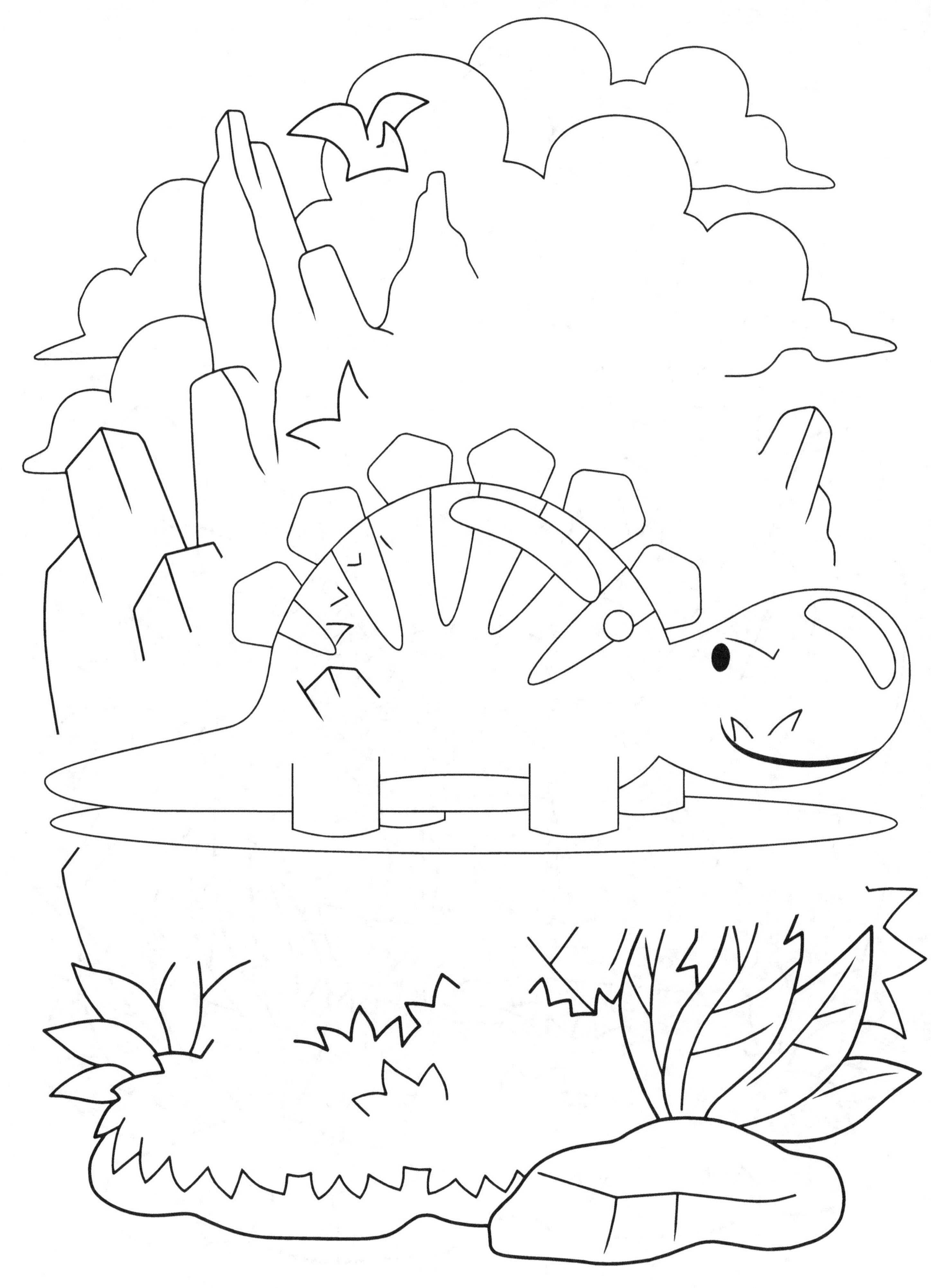

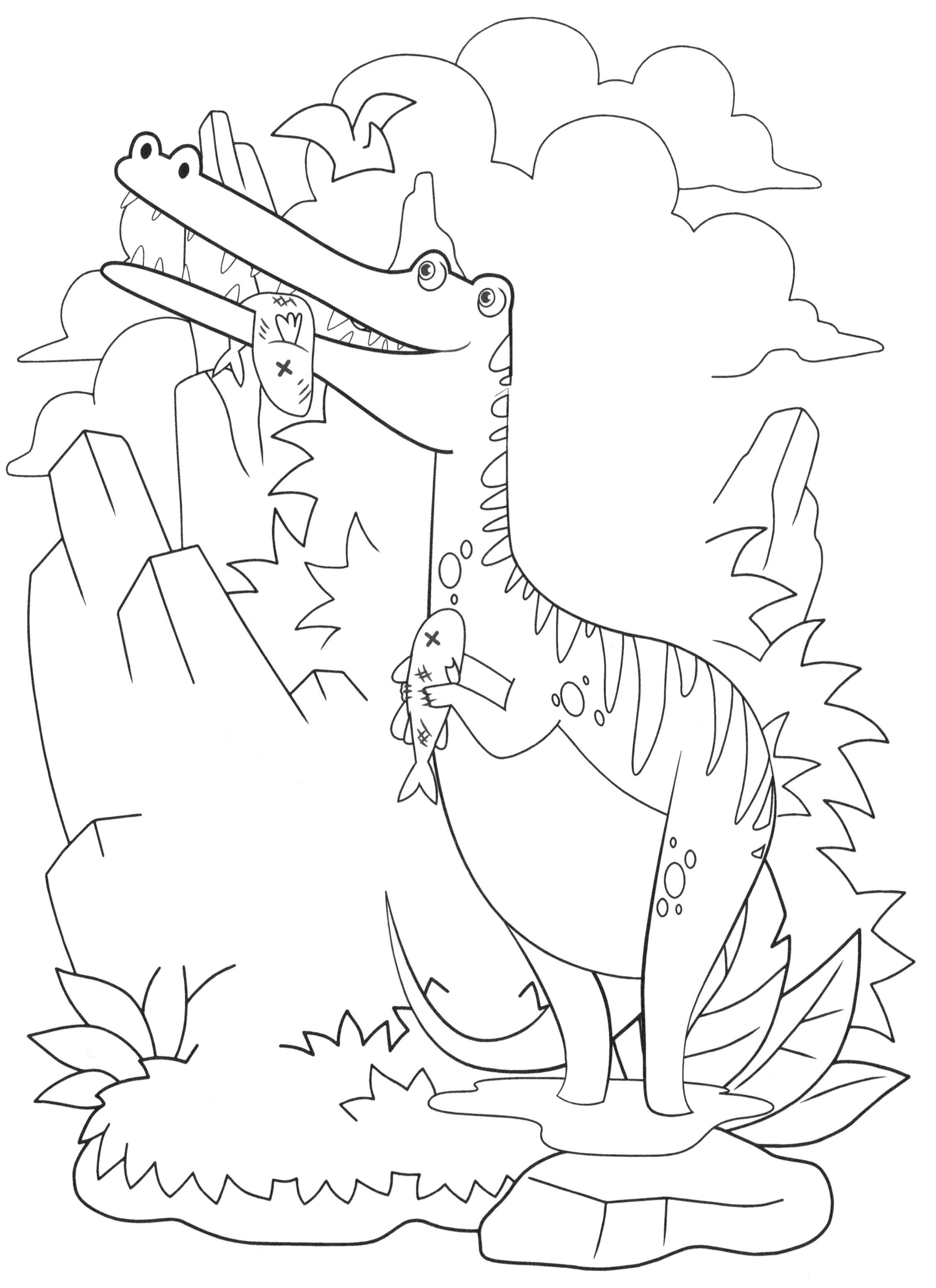

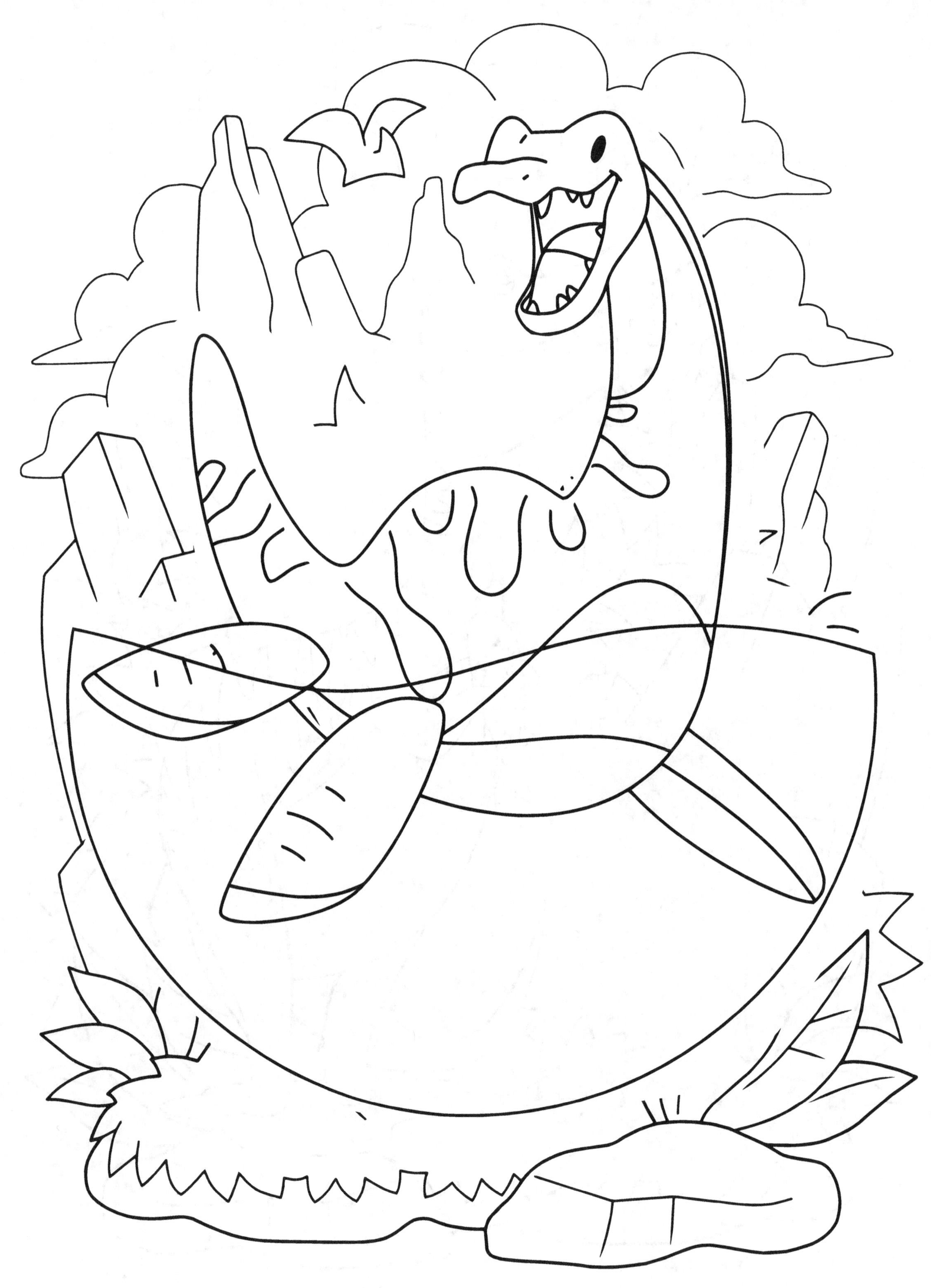

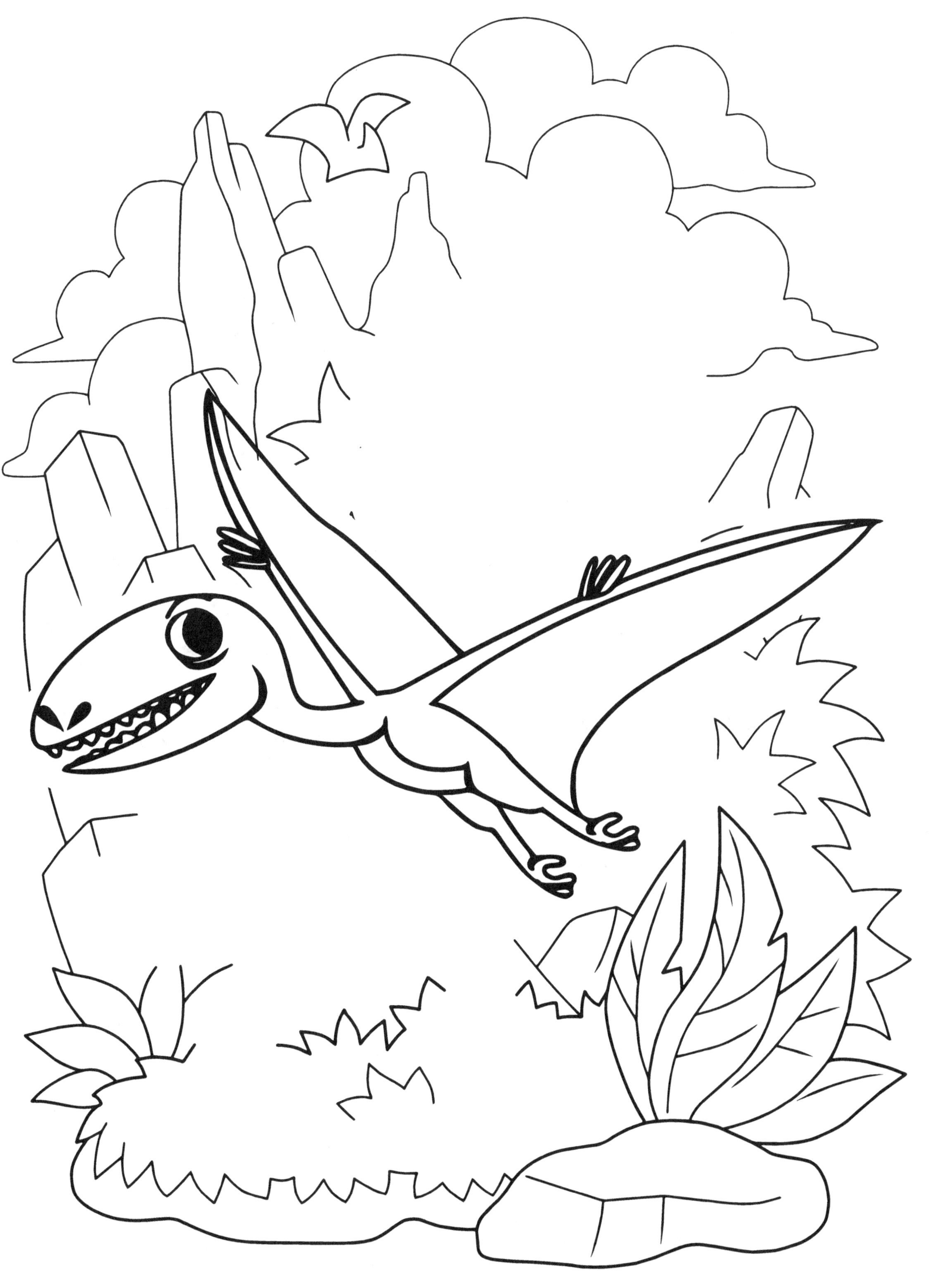

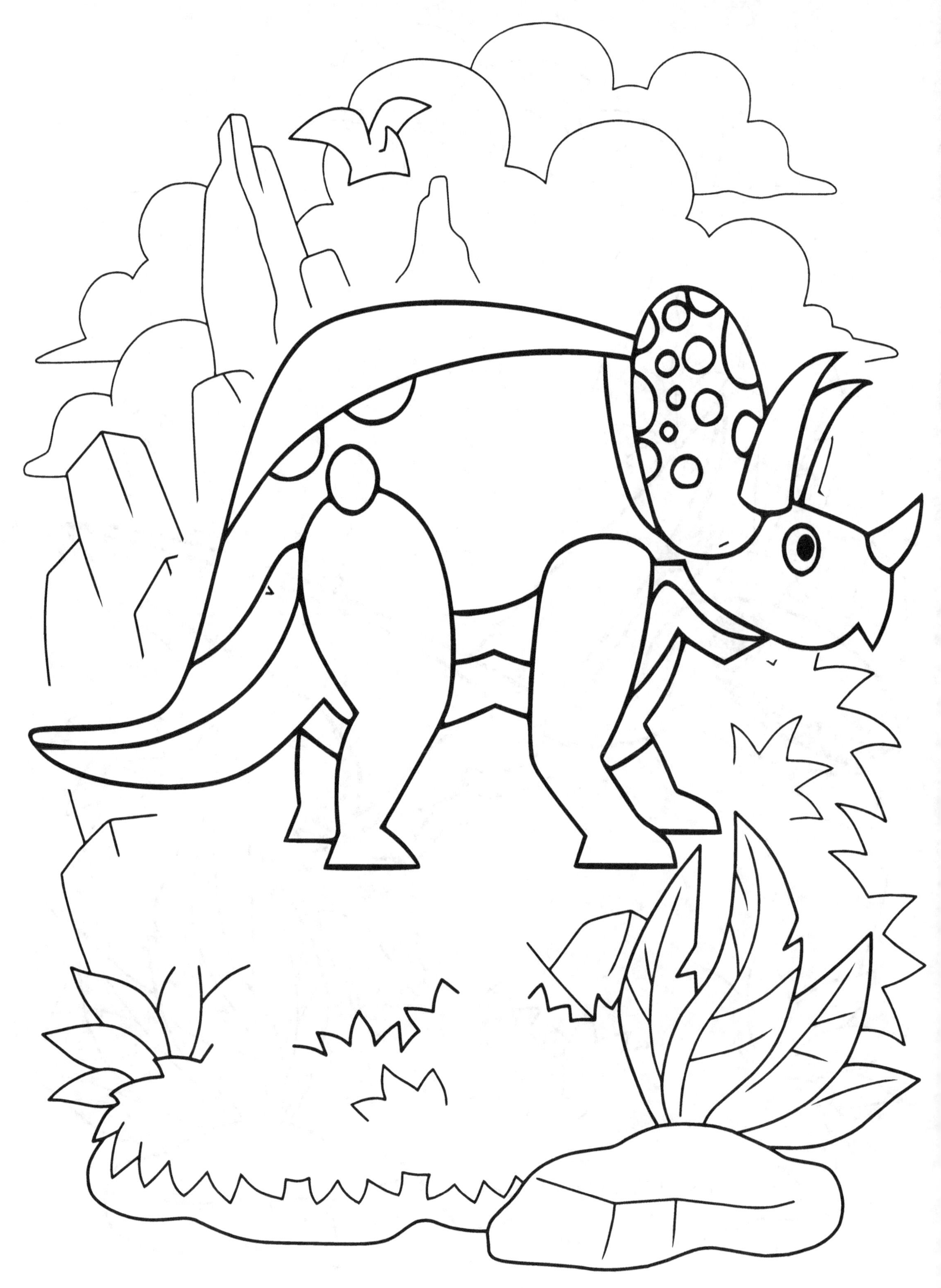

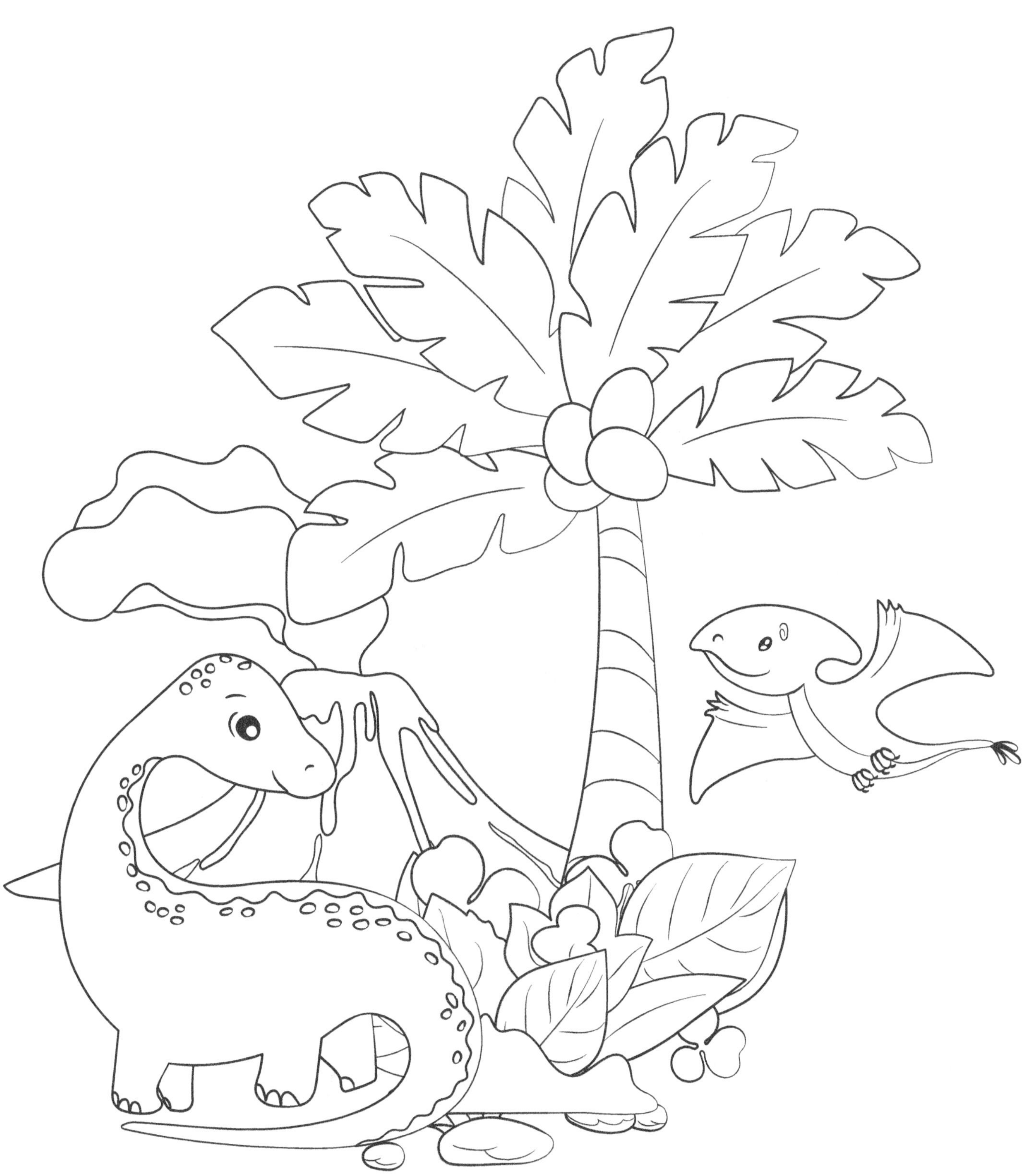

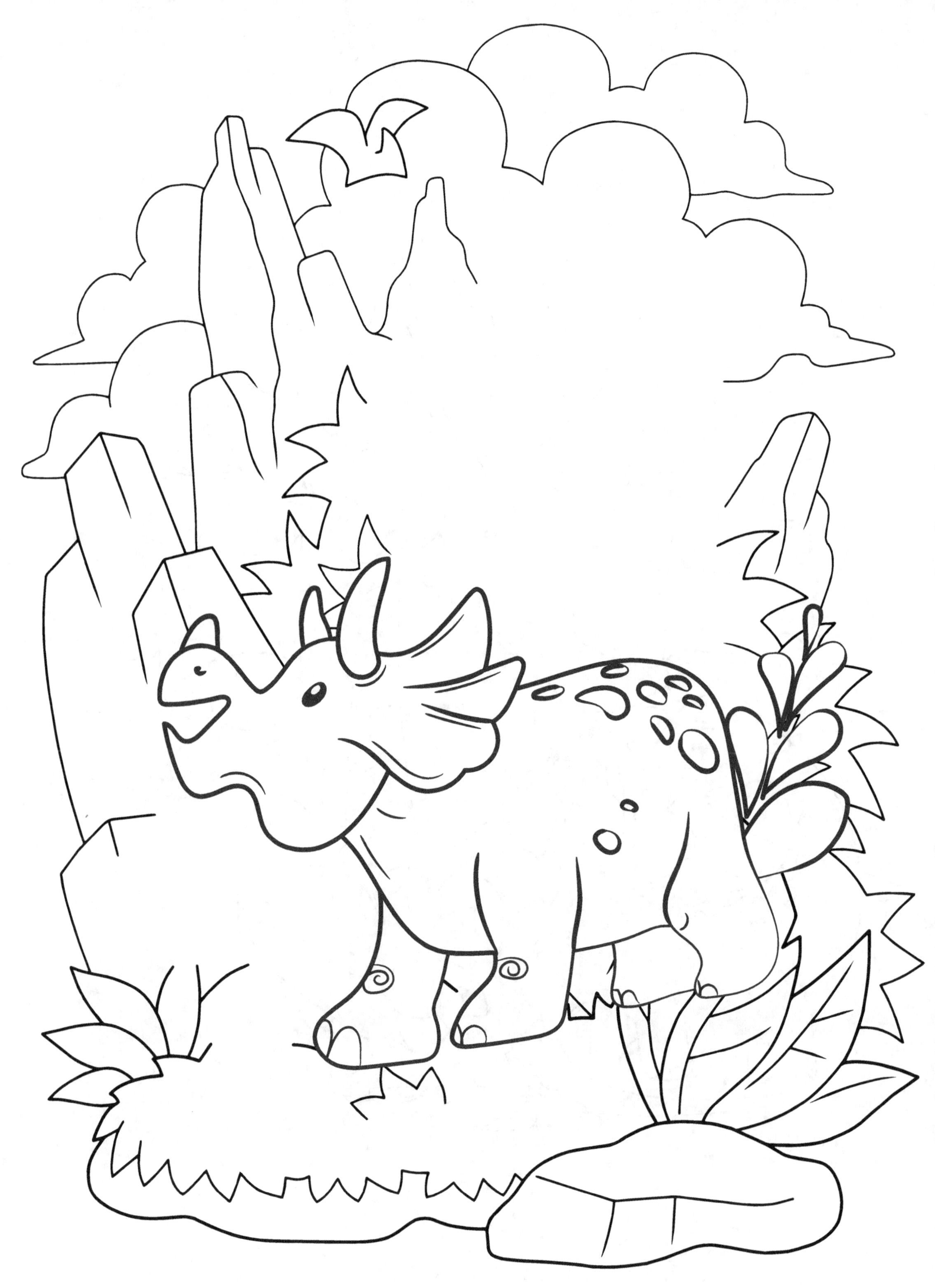

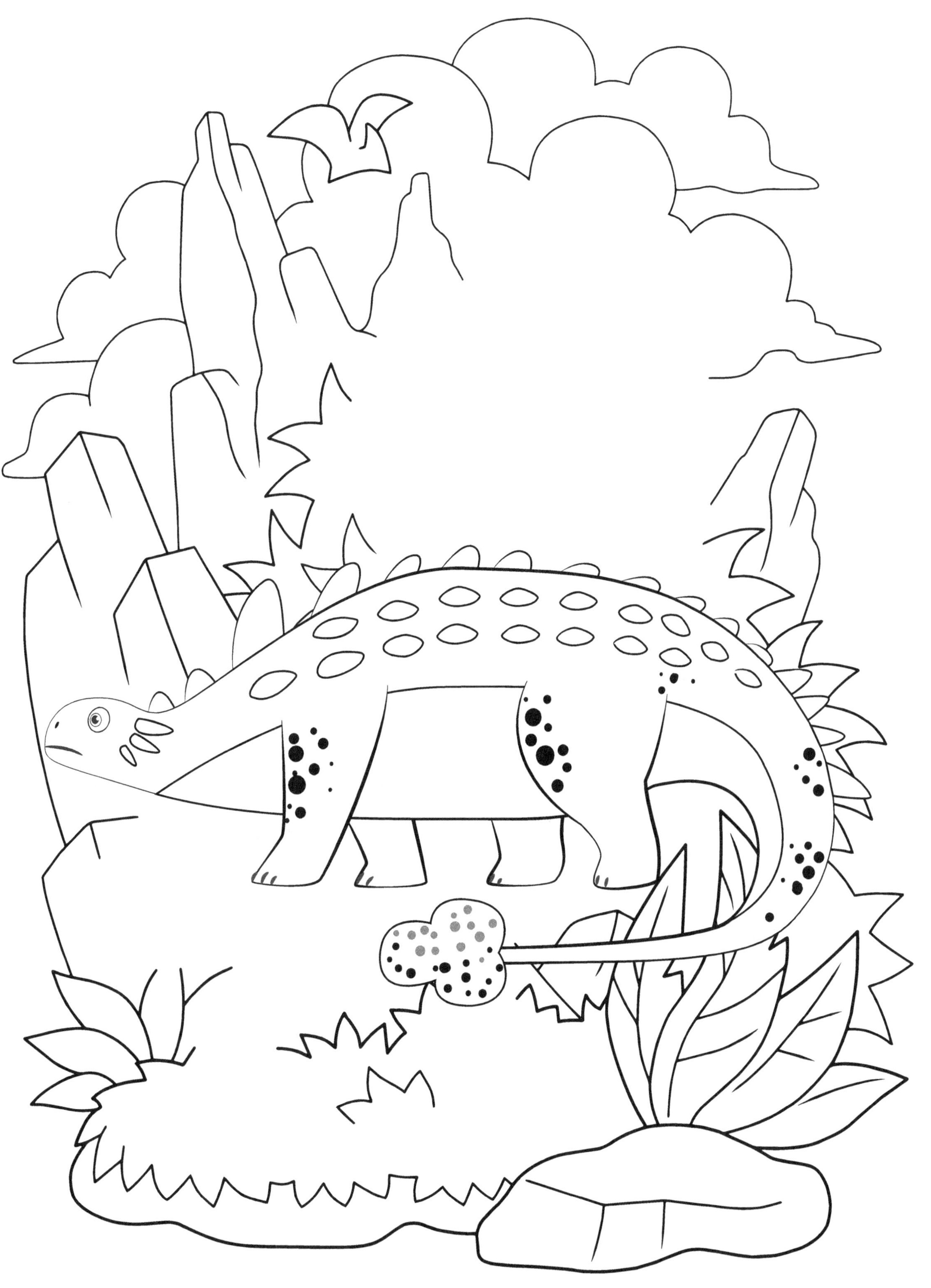

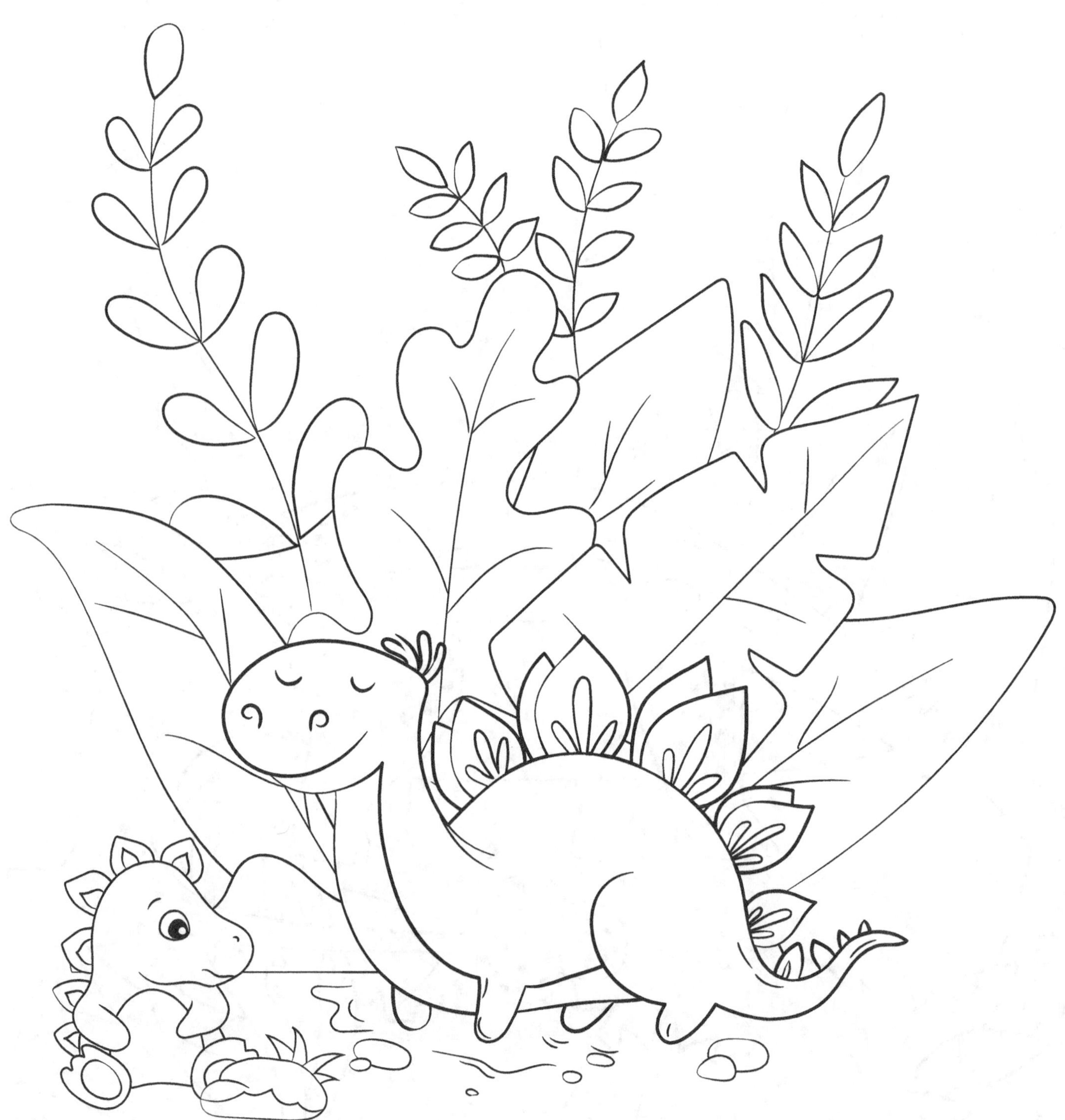

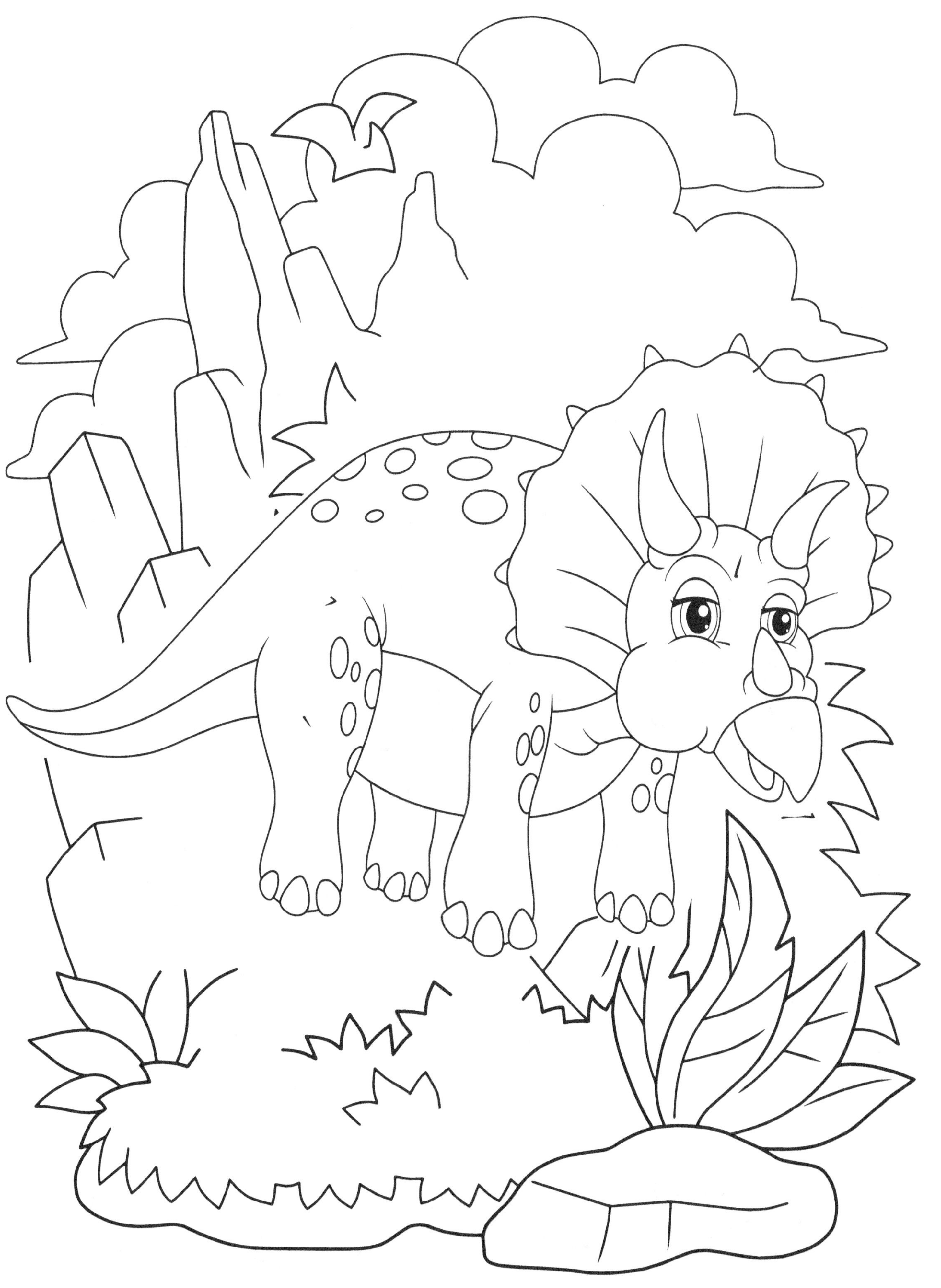

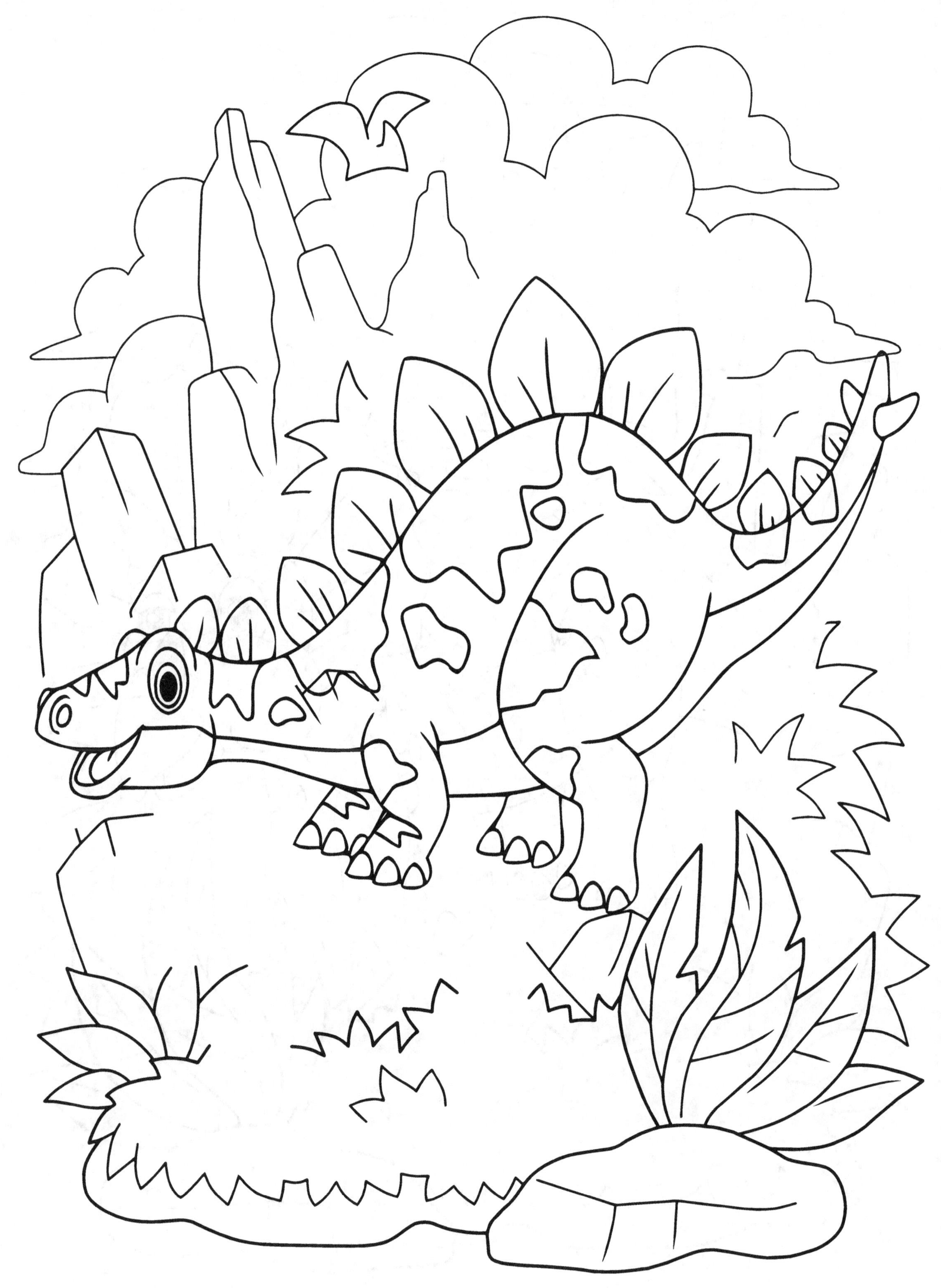

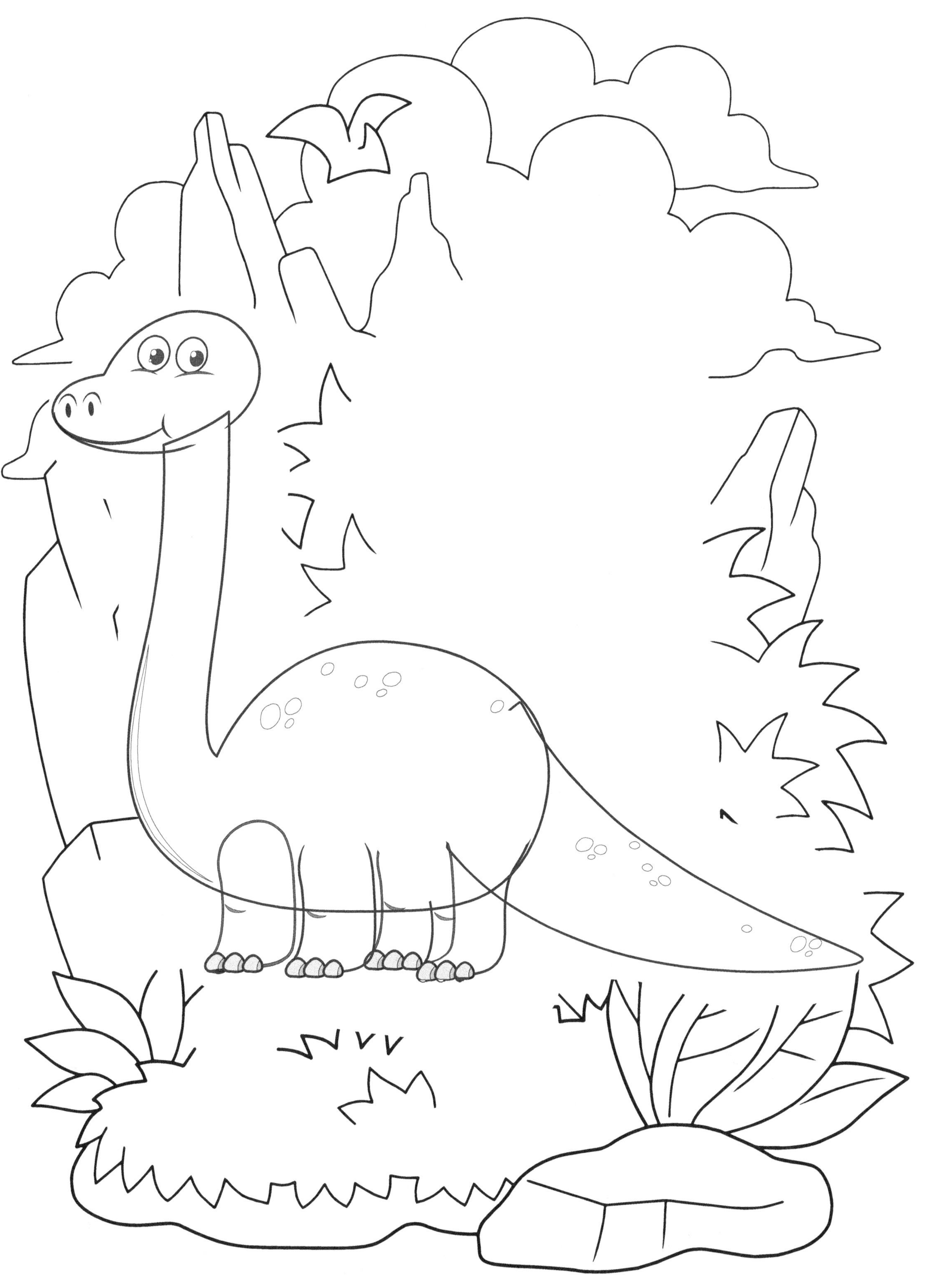

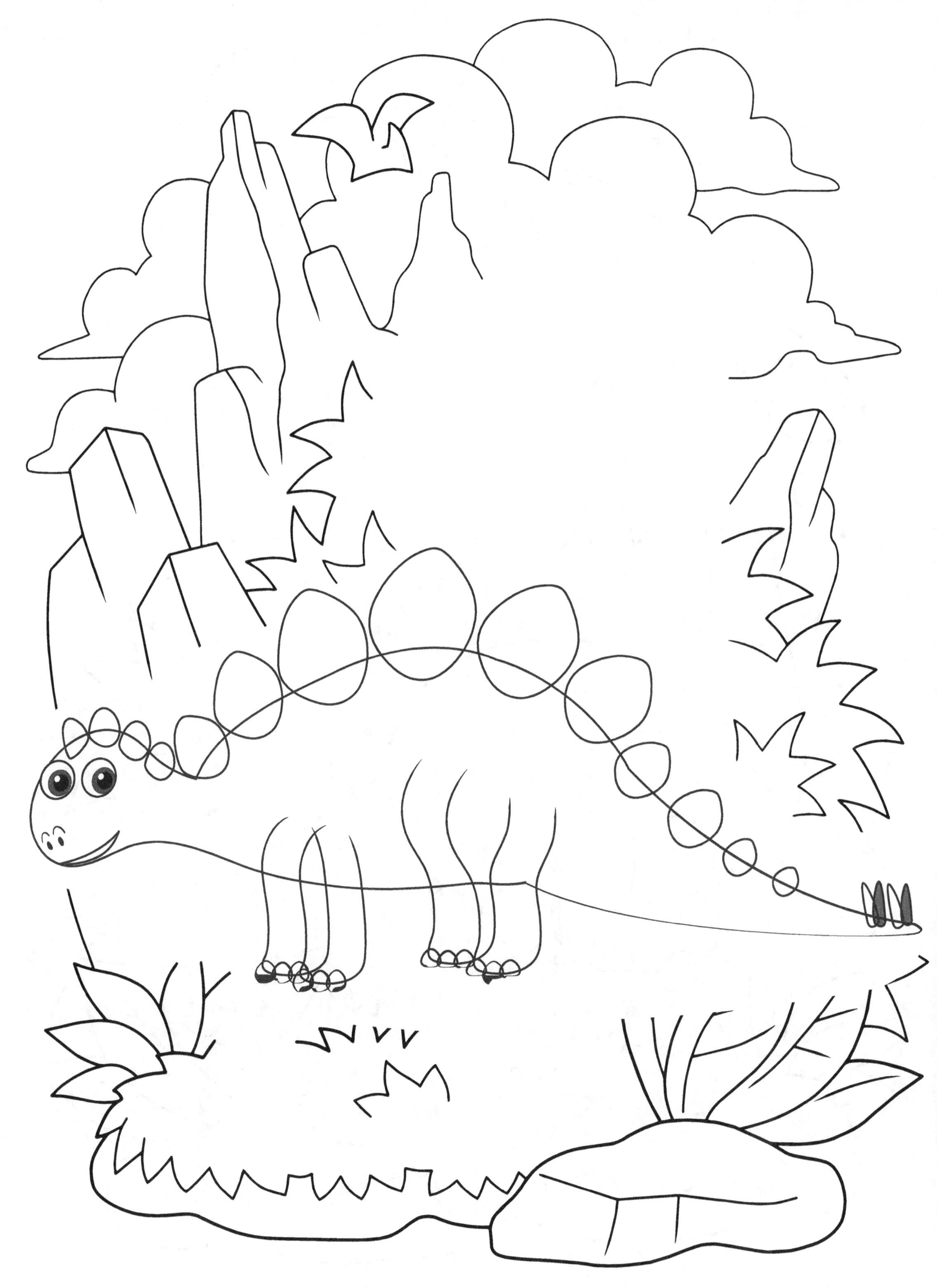

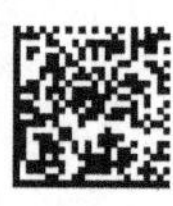